Advance Prai

"In a time when educators are examining their own relationships with education technology, *Tech for Teacher Wellness* offers a thoughtful perspective for the reader. I love how Meredith presents practical suggestions for daily self-care, creating boundaries, and staying energized in our profession. With a focus on supportive ideas like 'digital positivity' and 'remixing' lessons, this is a perfect and timely title to add to any teacher's bookshelf!

—Jennifer Williams, Author of
Teach Boldly: Using Edtech for Social Good, ISTE

"*Tech for Teacher Wellness* is an amazing book that speaks to educators. If you are a teacher who desires some tips on how to balance your career and personal life through tech resources, this book is for you. This book is jam-packed with everything you need to create the best balance. Meredith's insight will help you become more efficient in all aspects of your life. This is the book that you've been waiting for to give you everything that you need to bring you to teacher wellness. You will forever be referring to this book!

—Misty Savario, First Grade ITEC teacher,
2015 LACUE Elementary Teacher of the Year

"I wish I'd had this book thirteen years ago during my early career as an educator. Meredith presents an array of invaluable tools and thought-provoking challenges, and her extensive teaching experience shines through her words. This book will strike a chord with educators of diverse backgrounds and levels of experience, and all of them will identify at least one facet of this text that will profoundly resonate and prove instrumental in their professional journey."

—Marielle Wells,
Curriculum Developer and Creative Designer

"Embark on a wonderful journey to support teacher well-being with *Tech for Teacher Wellness*. This incredible book takes educators through a holistic approach, helping them evaluate their job satisfaction and cultivate a positive digital mindset. Each chapter is filled with reflection opportunities and QR codes for easy access to additional resources. It empowers teachers to prioritize self-care, set boundaries, and boost their efficiency. You won't want to miss out on this essential guide for a healthy and rewarding teaching career.

—Jeni Long,
Edtech Consultant, Speaker, Author

Tech for Teacher Wellness

Strategies for a Healthy Life and Sustainable Career

Meredith Masar Boullion

International Society for Technology in Education

ARLINGTON, VIRGINIA

Director of Books and Journals: *Emily Reed*
Acquisitions Editor: *Valerie Witte*
Editor: *Stephanie Argy*
Copy Editor: *Joanna Szabo*
Proofreader: *Emily Padgett*
Indexer: *Kento Ikeda*
Book Design and Production: *Olivia M. Hammerman*
Cover Design: *Christina DeYoung*

Names: Boullion, Meredith Masar, author.
Title: Tech for teacher wellness : strategies for a healthy life and sustainable career / Meredith Masar Boullion.
Description: First edition. | Portland, Oregon : International Society for Technology in Education, 2023. | Includes bibliographical references and index.
Identifiers: LCCN 2023024712 (print) | LCCN 2023024713 (ebook) | ISBN 9781564849991 (paperback) | ISBN 9798888370001 (epub) | ISBN 9798888370018 (pdf)
Subjects: LCSH: Teachers—Mental health. | Teachers—Job stress. | Teachers—Job satisfaction. | Teachers—Professional relationships. | Stress management. | Work-life balanace. | Information technology—Psychological aspects.
Classification: LCC LB2840 .B684 2023 (print) | LCC LB2840 (ebook) | DDC 371.1—dc23/eng/20230715
LC record available at https://lccn.loc.gov/2023024712
LC ebook record available at https://lccn.loc.gov/2023024713

First Edition

ISBN: 978-1-56484-999-1

Ebook version available

Printed in the United States of America

ISTE® is a registered trademark of the International Society for Technology in Education.

Contents

About ISTE

THE INTERNATIONAL SOCIETY FOR TECHNOLOGY IN EDUCATION (ISTE) IS home to a passionate community of global educators who believe in the power of technology to transform teaching and learning, accelerate innovation and solve tough problems in education.

ISTE inspires the creation of solutions and connections that improve opportunities for all learners by delivering: practical guidance, evidence-based professional learning, virtual networks, thought-provoking events and the ISTE Standards. ISTE is also the leading publisher of books focused on technology in education. For more information or to become an ISTE member, visit iste.org. Subscribe to ISTE's YouTube channel and connect with ISTE on X, Facebook, and LinkedIn.

RELATED ISTE TITLES

Pathways to Well-Being: Helping Educators (and Others) Find Balance in a Connected World, Susan Brooks-Young and Sara Armstrong (2018)

Stretch Yourself: A Personalized Journey to Deepen Your Teaching Practice, Caitlin McLemore and Fanny Passeport (2019)

Awesome Sauce: Creative Videos to Inspire Students, Engage Parents and Save You Time, Josh Stock (2020)

To see all books available from ISTE, please visit iste.org/books.

About the Author

MEREDITH MASAR BOULLION is a district technology facilitator who supports teachers with edtech integration. In her free time, she enjoys gardening, traveling, hiking, and undertaking home improvement projects that are most likely better left to the pros. She and her husband, Russell, have two daughters, Caroline and Annie. She holds a Bachelor of Science in Psychology from McNeese State University and a Master of Science in Instructional Media from Wilkes University. Meredith is a state-certified Louisiana Technology Facilitator, an ISTE-Certified Educator, a member of the Louisiana Association of Computer Using Educators (LACUE), a member of the Texas Computer Educator Association (TCEA), and a Microsoft Innovative Educator Expert (MIEE).

Acknowledgments

Publisher Acknowledgments

ISTE gratefully acknowledges the contributions of the following:

ISTE Standards Reviewers: Jackie Patanio, Tiffanie Zaugg

Manuscript Reviewers: Kyle M. Dunbar, Cammie Kannekens, Lisa A. Kuhn-Oldiges, Kristy Nelson, Michelle Palmieri, Hue-An Wren

Author Acknowledgments

The author wishes to acknowledge and express appreciation to the following:

Her entire family who provides understanding and encouragement, especially Russell, Caroline, and Annie.

Her friends who give her advice, support, and excused absences from socializing while working on this project.

The Tritechta for their continued support and encouragement.

CPSB Chief Technology Officer, Kim Leblanc, who provides opportunities for professional growth and encouragement.

Educators who work hard every day to make a positive difference in the lives of their students.

The editorial and design staff at ISTE Books, especially Stephanie Argy and Valerie Witte.

For my mother, Carolyn Masar, who would have been incredibly proud and thrilled to know that the book idea pitched to her in an infusion room at MD Anderson has come to fruition.

Preface

WHEN I BEGAN TEACHING IN 2000, MY DEAR AUNT GENIE, A RETIRED elementary teacher, was so excited. She remarked, "Teaching is a great way of life." Her words reassured me as I transitioned into a new career in education. What I couldn't yet understand back then was that teaching quickly takes over one's life. I woke up thinking about my students and what needed to be ready for the day. I spent most weeknights grading and planning, with the events of each day on my mind while prepping for the next one to come. The boundaries between my work life and personal life began to diminish. And to be honest, I didn't even mind because I loved what I did and just thought it was part of the job.

After spending seven years teaching science in a middle school classroom and another seven teaching high school biology and English, I took a position as a district technology facilitator. In this role since 2014, I have been fortunate to be able to provide support for teachers with edtech integration, which is also tremendously rewarding. The integration of tech to support teaching and learning has impacted education in positive ways, with features that make content accessible, differentiate learning, provide collaborative experiences, and streamline classroom efficiency; however, other aspects of technology have created stressors that could use a new type of edtech support: tech to support teacher wellness.

While most careers have experienced a blurring of the boundaries between work and personal life due to technology, I see the toll it can take specifically on my teacher friends, making a demanding career even more so. Now, with constant access to email, lessons, student work, and grades, there are no boundaries; work and personal lives have overlapped to become life. Teachers wearily respond to email after hours and on weekends, grade lessons while riding in a car, and provide feedback on assignments while waiting in lines at the store. In this connected world, teachers always have access to work, often within arm's reach. When they choose to participate in social media like many normal folks, they can find themselves subject to scrutiny in ways not previously possible or spiraling down rabbit holes that amplify feelings of stress or negativity.

Maintaining a personal identity outside of being a teacher is perfectly okay to do—in fact, it provides life balance and a reduction in stress. The loss of self, coupled with existing in an ever-connected constant state of work mode is a blueprint for anxiety, cynicism, and burnout. While the current state of education as a career choice is suffering, a diminished sense of emotional well-being will only exacerbate the issue. By no means am I suggesting that this book is a cure for all that ails teachers. It is simply a book of suggestions presented in the hope that you might choose to integrate them throughout your career, no matter in which stage you are today. Through your reading experience, I hope you discover practical tech strategies and resources to help you achieve a greater sense of well-being.

Introduction

FEW WOULD ARGUE AGAINST SUPPORTING THE EMOTIONAL WELL-BEING of students, and rightly so. In fact, teachers are often the strongest advocates for it. But it is also time to acknowledge and address the emotional wellness of teachers. Just as it is a challenge for a student to learn when in a negative emotional state, it is also a challenge for a teacher to meet the demands of their job when they are in distress.

While multiple factors come into play for the reasons surrounding teacher stress and career dissatisfaction, this book specifically addresses how a post-pandemic digital shift in education has become an occupational stressor for teachers. It provides practical resources and strategies for educators to integrate to:

- become more self-aware regarding their feelings and attitudes toward teaching and technology

- develop self-care strategies to adopt as habits

- practice mindfulness and breathing skills to calm classroom anxieties

- use technology to establish healthy work and home life boundaries

- foster and promote digital positivity

- use tech features to be more efficient

- remain engaged in teaching and learning

To gain insight into the science of teacher wellness, a paper entitled *Interventions Fostering Well-Being of Schoolteachers: A Review of Research* acknowledges that while there is a need to support this topic of research, educational interventions to support teachers are most effective when they are provided as practical solutions that can be implemented directly in the classroom (Dreer & Gouasé, 2021). Teachers have little time to spend in training, so they need support that is relevant and easily integrated. Therefore, the purpose of this book is to provide tech strategies that can be implemented directly to make a positive impact on one's emotional well-being and foster a greater sense of career satisfaction.

Tech Strategies as Seeds

In chapters 2 through 6, consider the numbered practical tech strategies as "seeds" provided to help your teaching garden blossom throughout your career. These seeds are suggestions to integrate, with the goal of producing healthy growth to bloom and bear fruit, but by no means is it intended or expected for you to integrate them all. You can enjoy a bountiful harvest by sowing your own select choice of seeds.

ISTE Standards

The ISTE Standards provide a framework for this book's content and are noted as sidebars where relevant.

The **ISTE Standards for Education Leaders** indicate suggestions for how teachers can reach their full growth potential with administrative support.

The **ISTE Standards for Coaches** indicate suggestions for how coaches can provide what teachers need through professional development and support to nurture teacher growth.

The **ISTE Standards for Educators** indicate when the strategies or seeds support teacher integration of technology. Through the cultivation of these seeds, teachers may become companion plants, providing an optimally healthy school environment through modeling, and guidance for other teachers.

Chapter Reflections

At the end of chapters 2–6, there are reflection pages that provide chapter-related questions to ponder and prompts to consider. These reflection questions can be used for personal journaling, professional coaching or mentoring, or to guide small group discussions for professional development or book clubs.

Sketchnote Pages

At the end of each chapter, after you have the opportunity to reflect on the chapter content, there is a page available for sketchnoting. This is place to consider which strategies you intend to integrate and illustrate the ways in which you anticipate applying the chapter's strategies, or which seeds to plant, and to consider your goals or desired growth of the seeds you choose to sow. Consider what types of support you anticipate needing to meet your potential, including how leaders and coaches can nurture your growth. There is plenty of space for you to imagine how the benefits you gain from growth will impact others. Also, consider how the fruits and blooms will yield benefits to others in your life, including family, friends, and students.

Interactive and Collaborative Activities

Opportunities are available to contribute to interactive activities to serve as reader repositories of collective resources. These activities are found in chapters 2 and 3.

Sharing on Social Media

While suggestions are made in chapter reflections for sharing on social media, readers are also encouraged to do so when ideas or strategies make a meaningful and positive impact.

If sharing an idea or strategy, use the #teacherwellness to raise awareness. Feel free to tag me, @realtechfored, on X, Instagram or Threads as well. Share any ideas, strategies, or reflections you feel comfortable sharing on social media. Use the hashtag #teacherwellness to raise awareness. Feel free to tag me, @ realtechfored, on Instagram, Threads, or X.

Chapter 1

How Are You Doing?

"I am satisfied with my role in the classroom, but I am beyond exhausted by how much has been added to our duties without providing more time for planning and preparation."
—Sarun, a Louisiana high school teacher
with 25+ years of experience as an educator

The Act of Teaching is Satisfying and Rewarding

Teachers genuinely find great satisfaction when:

- they can successfully teach their students to become proficient in whatever subject matter they teach.

- the positive social skills they teach, model, and reinforce are adopted as behaviors in their students.

- they provide experiences for students to strengthen their cognitive critical thinking and design thinking skills and can see student growth.

- students beautifully express their creativity when provided with the opportunity to do so.

Indeed, when teachers are asked about job satisfaction, they have no trouble finding it when it comes to their interactions with students because the act of teaching is satisfying and rewarding. But being a teacher is not only about teaching—and finding satisfaction in the other parts of the job can be more of a challenge.

Locus of Control in the Classroom

Locus of control is a concept developed by American psychologist Julian B. Rotter during the 1950s and 1960s. It refers to a person's perception of the degree to which internal versus external forces influence the outcomes in their life (Rotter, 1966). Those who perceive a stronger sense of an internal locus of control, or lack of external influence, tend to have more favorable perceptions regarding their abilities to positively affect outcomes. And those who perceive a stronger sense of external locus of control, or low internal control, tend to have less favorable perceptions regarding their ability to impact outcomes (Rotter, 1966).

The factors that influence teaching, beyond the interactions between teacher and student, are many and vary by teacher, school, department, district, state, and country. Ever-changing classroom management needs, varying social and behavioral situations, subject area standardized test obligations, administrative demands, district expectations, legal requirements, and federal regulations all have the potential to chip away at a teacher's sense of autonomy.

INTERNAL LOCUS OF CONTROL vs **EXTERNAL LOCUS OF CONTROL**

- teacher autonomy
- not feeling micromanaged
- minimal teaching disruptions
- minimal non-teaching obligations
- minimal parent/guardian inquiries
- professional development choices
- healthy work/personal life boundaries

- lack of flexibility in curriculum
- feeling micromanaged
- persistent class disruptions
- multiple non-teaching obligations
- persistent parent/guardian demands
- no professional development choice
- unhealthy work/personal life boundaries

External demands persist at every moment of every day, and each day brings new expectations and stressors. The multitude of external influences as depicted in the illustration lend themselves to create a diminished sense of an internal locus of control in teaching, thus reducing one's sense of autonomy. This sense of diminished internal control helps explain why so many teachers find satisfaction with their interactions with students while expressing less satisfaction with their career.

External demands are constant, ever-changing, and determined by a variety of factors including technology integration. This book considers the single influence of technology and how some of the features of it can be leveraged in order to improve a sense of well-being.

> When tech coaches plan professional development for teachers, consider **ISTE Standard for Coaches 4.5.a**, which asks coaches to "design professional learning based on needs assessments and frameworks for working with adults to support their cultural, social-emotional and learning needs." When doing so, the emotional needs of the teacher are to be considered and the training designed to accommodate their needs. If, as a teacher, you would like this to happen, reach out to the tech coaches who support you and communicate what you need. Coaches are an integral component of the teacher support system.

Technology as an External Influence

Inundating teachers with new technologies that they are expected to integrate into their classrooms is one major external factor which can create a diminished sense of internal control. In the current environment, we need to be cautious in our expectations that the windfall of newly acquired edtech granted by post-pandemic investments will be immediately impactful and transformative. It will take a shared vision of leaders, meaningful and relevant technology training, time, and consideration for teacher wellness in order for technology to truly transform teaching and learning.

Once teachers acclimate to new digital environments and learn how to meaningfully use the tools they now have, they will regain a greater sense of internal control when it comes to edtech integration. This factor can contribute to shifting teacher autonomy and lay the groundwork for digital transformation in education.

Technology Integration Mindset

Before teachers become proficient and master tech integration to promote higher thinking skills, an internal sense of control is the key foundation upon which this growth can occur. Mindset theory (Dweck & Leggett, 1988) is a social cognitive approach to motivation and personality. The concept of fostering a growth mindset in learners is held in high regard and widely accepted. Holding a growth mindset means that when one believes they can improve their proficiency or intelligence and take ownership over their own growth, they have a greater likelihood of reaching their goals. Chapter 7 in Dweck's *Mindset, The New Psychology of Success: How We Can Learn to Fulfill our Potential* contains information for parents, teachers, and coaches. She addresses how people with good intentions send children messages that undermine growth mindset. She goes on to illustrate how to frame praise and criticism in ways that develop the growth mindset instead (Dweck, 2007).

If one believes that they are in control of the trajectory of their learning, they are more likely to experience success. This happens every day in classrooms when students are encouraged to set personal learning goals which they reflect upon and modify depending on their progress. It makes sense for the same to be true of teachers and tech integration learning goals. Many teachers I have spoken to start with a statement about how "bad" or "nervous" they are with technology. District and school leaders, and especially tech coaches, should consider how to work with teachers in ways that foster a growth mindset. Meaningful and effective edtech integration takes practice, lots of plan Bs, and patience.

Teachers, like students, benefit from feeling a sense of control over their own learning paths when it comes to tech integration. One size does not fit all, which is why offering teachers choice in their professional development (PD) is one way to provide them with what they need. Too many teachers have grown weary of in-services that are geared either far above or far below their proficiency. If not already available, teachers should express their interest in more options like differentiated micro courses, on-demand resources, and focused content. Flexibility and teacher choice for edtech PD should be offered to support teachers and allow them to take ownership over their learning.

> When tech coaches and teachers work together on individual PD goals and objectives, the learning is personalized and aligns to the **ISTE Standard for Coaches 4.1.c,**which recommends that coaches "cultivate a supportive coaching culture that encourages educators and leaders to achieve a shared vision and individual goals." If you currently feel like coaches are not quite meeting your needs, reach out and ask them to help you develop individual goals and objectives to support your needs.

> The teamwork between tech coaches and educators to individualize a PD plan supports the **ISTE Standard for Educators 2.1.a** which suggests that educators "set professional learning goals to explore and apply pedagogical approaches made possible by technology and reflect on their effectiveness." With this approach, teachers can control the integration of the technology available to them and their students, and use that technology to support learning goals.

The Power of Tech to Transform Education

Technology, in the hands of teachers who embrace its ability to positively impact the teaching and learning experience, has the power to transform education. There is no time like the present to recognize this potential, with incredible investments being made in educational technology, along with the prospect of innovative emerging technologies like artificial intelligence (AI). Technology gives teachers and students opportunities to connect and collaborate in meaningful ways, and it allows teachers and students to become curators and creators of content rather than remain passive consumers.

In 2021, researchers at the University of Seville published a literature review to learn more about the impact that edtech has on teacher stress and anxiety. At the time of the review, only sixteen studies had been published on this subject between the years 2005–2019. The study found that teachers have high levels of anxiety or stress regarding the use of edtech—and that this anxiety has "grown exponentially over time." One item of note in the study's conclusion states that "training is essential to achieve a professionalization of teachers with sufficient capacity to combat the challenges of instructional processes." (Fernández-Batanero et al., 2021). In other words, inundating classrooms with laptops, Chromebooks, and other devices does not guarantee a transformation of education for the better. It is essential that proper training be provided as well.

> Districts and leaders should have a plan for the technology integrated in the school system. The **ISTE Standard for Education Leaders 3.2 Visionary Planner** calls for them to "engage others in establishing a vision, strategic plan and ongoing evaluation cycle for transforming learning with technology." If you are uncertain about the objectives and direction in which technology integration is headed in your situation, reach out to school and district leaders to see if a strategic plan is available to review.

> Teachers are responsible for the culture and climate in the classroom. The **ISTE Standard for Coaches 4.5 Professional Learning Facilitator** calls for coaches "to design professional learning based on needs assessments and frameworks for working with adults to support their cultural, social-emotional and learning needs." If you are feeling overwhelmed, lost, or frustrated, be sure to communicate these feelings to your tech coach. Don't be afraid to ask for what you need.

Chapter 1 Reflections

Consider the content provided in chapter 1 and take a moment to reflect on the following prompts. These prompts can be used individually, with a small group, or in a book club.

- How do you perceive your own locus of control as it relates to the classroom? Do you think that you have autonomy to impact student learning, or do you feel as though external factors have a greater impact?

- Consider ISTE Standard for Educators 2.1.a, which encourages educators to "set professional learning goals to explore and apply pedagogical approaches made possible by technology and reflect on their effectiveness." What sorts of learning goals do you have in mind? In your experiences, what have been the most effective edtech integration experiences to impact student learning?

- Do you have any choice regarding your own professional development? If not, do you have a way of providing input to effect change that you would like to experience?

- Do you see yourself making a career of being an educator? What support do you think you need to be able to do so?

  _____

  _____

  _____

  _____

Share any reflections or thoughts that you feel comfortable sharing on social media with the hashtag #SupportTeacherWellness to raise public awareness. Tag @realtechfored in your post.

Chapter 2

Well-Being

"I love tech and finding new ways to engage students, but it can be overwhelming."
—Lisa, a Texas elementary teacher
with 6–10 years of experience as an educator

THIS CHAPTER EXPLORES THE IMPORTANCE OF TAKING A MOMENT TO acknowledge your current state of job satisfaction. Teacher well-being impacts student learning. Becoming self-aware to identify any feelings of stress or anxiety is a first step toward seeking a greater sense of emotional wellness—both for yourself and your students.

The Impact of Teacher Well-Being on Students

Even if the state of education before the COVID pandemic had been acceptable, with fair teacher pay, strong feelings of autonomy, and reasonable work expectations, teachers would still have felt a heightened sense of occupational stress caused by the influx of new technology. Teachers, like their students, experienced high levels of trauma and loss both during and after the pandemic. Many, carrying their own grief and stress, returned to the classroom to find students with monumental gaps in learning who were struggling to re-socialize and acclimate back to the classroom environment.

In a 2021 Finnish study published in the *International Journal of School & Educational Psychology*, researchers found that stress and burnout experienced by teachers crosses over and impacts the emotional well-being of students (Tikkanen et al., 2021). If teachers remain in a heightened state of stress and feel burnout, it can have a ripple effect, passing on to students and potentially other teachers. If teachers become frustrated and cynical about edtech, it has the potential to become an undermining factor in edtech integration. School leaders and coaches have a responsibility to foster the well-being of teachers. It is not something that teachers should be expected to address and correct in isolation.

Occupational Stress and Technostress in Education

Occupational stress is defined as a mismatch between the expectations and demands of a job with a person's capacity and ability to do the job. With so many new technological advances in such a short amount of time, many teachers have not been afforded the time or opportunity to learn how to use all the new resources provided. In most cases, teachers are not opposed to using these resources; they are simply overwhelmed by all the new options and have not had ample time to learn how to best use them. Teachers need to be given time and varied professional development opportunities that meet their diverse needs to learn how to manage and integrate the tools with which they have been provided.

According to the American Psychological Association dictionary, techno-stress is "a form of occupational stress that is associated with information and communication technologies such as the internet, mobile devices, and social media. . . . This relatively new phenomenon has significant detrimental effects on individuals' health, productivity, and work satisfaction and has been proposed as an important predictor of overall job strain." In 2020, a team of researchers published the results of a study to investigate the impact that two types of technostress—techno-anxiety and techno-fatigue—have on Chilean teachers. Techno-anxiety occurs when a working person experiences high levels of distress, tension, or discomfort from the use of information and communication technology. This type of anxiety is believed to lead to skepticism about technology integration, including negative attitudes regarding one's own competence and abilities to use the tech. Techno-fatigue refers to feelings of mental and cognitive exhaustion and overload due to information fatigue. This type of fatigue is considered to lead to an inability to organize and synthesize new information. The study determined that 13% of teachers presented a techno-anxiety condition and 12% experienced techno-fatigued conditions (Estrada-Muñoz et al., 2020). Note that this study was published in May of 2020, still relatively early in the pandemic.

Technology Stressors for Teachers

Occupational Stressors

- expectations for managing 1:1 learning environments
- providing virtual options
- balancing virtual & face-to-face environments
- expectations to utilize newly adopted remediation tools with fidelity
- teaching students how to use all of the above before feeling proficient themselves

Technostressors

- email volume
- email management
- expectations for processing large amounts of information through email messages
- digital notifications
- steady stream of information
- online negativity
- social media scrutiny
- 24-7 access to all of the above

Teachers are currently facing a confluence of occupational stress and technostress. It's no wonder many schools and districts are experiencing diminished teacher enthusiasm for investing time and effort into learning how to use and integrate new tools and resources.

Declining Teacher Emotional Well-Being across the Globe

A decline in the emotional well-being of educators is an issue around the world. The Education and Solidarity Network (ESN) is a global nonprofit organization that believes "the health and well-being of education workers are vital factors for building quality education systems. To help promote the health and well-being of teachers at work, ESN carries out with its members and partners international surveys on the theme of health at work and a barometer of the health and well-being of education personnel" (Education and Solidarity Network, 2023).

Between May and July 2021, the ESN collected data from several thousand educators from six different international locations including Belgium, France, Mexico, Morocco, The Gambia, and Quebec, Canada. The table below illustrates the locations with educators who reported the highest percentages of the feelings and attitudes measured from the *ESN International Barometer of Health and Well-Being of Education Personnel Report*. The results as they relate to feelings of well-being are alarming.

Locations with highest percentages of teachers who reported that they often, very often, or always experience negative feelings such as anxiety, depression, and hopelessness include:		
France—52%	Belgium—46%	Quebec—35%
Locations with highest reported percentages of teachers who consider their work "somewhat" or "very" stressful since the beginning of the 2020–21 school year include:		
France—81%	Quebec, Canada—70%	Belgium—67%
Locations of highest reported percentages of teachers who have the impression that being a teacher is "not" or "not at all" valued in society include:		
Belgium—98%	France—97%	Quebec, Canada—91%
Locations with highest reported percentages of teachers who are dissatisfied with their work-life balance include:		
France—70%	Belgium—57%	Quebec—49%

Data Source: *ESN International Barometer of Health and Well-Being of Education Personnel Report* (Education and Solidarity Network, 2023)

In the United States, the National Education (NEA) commissioned a poll regarding stress and burnout in teachers. This survey collected data from more than 3,500 educators, and the results are no surprise. They found that 90% of respondents reported burnout as being a very or somewhat serious issue. More than half (55%) report that they intend to retire earlier than anticipated because of the pandemic (2022).

While the pandemic caused many consequences in education, its ripple effects continue to alter education. We find ourselves with a growing need for new teachers along with an increase in reported stress and burnout experienced by current teachers. The reasons for this situation vary by district, state, and country, but one thing remains true: systemic changes need to occur to improve both the wellness of teachers and, in turn, career sustainability.

Social-Emotional Learning (SEL)

Consider this passage from "Teaching Is Not Martyrdom" by Ryan Fan:

> Good teachers manage their stress, get adequate sleep, and take care of themselves. School districts across the country have started embracing social-emotional learning (SEL) as a more culturally responsive, restorative, and less punitive way for students to manage emotions and conflict. SEL is likely the most common buzzword in the world of education right now. But according to McGraw-Hill, schools work better when teachers have strong social-emotional learning competencies too. Their classrooms start to have more positive behaviors and outcomes. ("Teaching Is Not Martyrdom," Ryan Fan, PsychologyToday.com, April 2021)

Social-emotional learning (SEL) is a critical component of human development. It is how humans learn to positively deal with emotions, maintain healthy relationships, manage disagreements, show empathy, and get along with others. According to the Collaborative for Academic, Social, and Emotional Learning (CASEL), which conducted a meta-analysis of 213 studies involving more than 270,000 students, there is evidence that providing SEL interventions improves students' academic performance, classroom behavior, and abilities to manage anxiety and depression (CASEL, 2023). Studies such as this one provide evidence that there is a need for social-emotional learning skill development to be included in the instructional day to benefit students. Teachers recognize the value in prioritizing the emotional well-being of their students. They understand that when a student is in emotional distress, learning becomes challenging, if not impossible.

Remaining in a state of emotional distress takes a toll on teachers as well. Being emotionally unwell is not only detrimental to one's health, it also makes doing one's job especially difficult. Providing teachers with their own social-emotional training and support may be as beneficial for them as it is for students. Effective strategies for supporting teacher wellness should be taken into consideration by school leaders to minimize teacher distress and improve career longevity. Suggestions and examples from districts and schools that have demonstrated their support for teacher wellness are provided in chapter 7, "Supporting Teachers."

Educator Well-Being Survey

To gain insights into teacher well-being and attitudes toward edtech integration, I created an Educator Well-Being Survey. At the time of writing, this survey has been shared across social media, at the 2022 Louisiana Association of Computer Using Educators (LACUE) Conference, at the 2023 Texas Computer Education Association (TCEA) Conference, and by word of mouth.

For each question in the survey, respondents were able to add an optional comment to provide justification for their responses. Here are some comments shared when asked about their own perceived job satisfaction.

LOW JOB SATISFACTION COMMENTS

"Never enough time to get the expected workload completed and the amount of expected paperwork increases each year; student discipline isn't consistent or we aren't supported by administrators; all of the 'extra' that takes away from teaching and prep time, like PLC and PBIS meetings, tracking and paperwork, duties, working ballgames, tutoring, etc." (teacher, 11–15 years experience)

"Most programs to increase student achievement are chosen by people that are not in the classroom, so programs fail. The cycle goes on with new programs each year. It is exhausting when your voice is not heard as an educator." (teacher, 16–20 years experience)

"Each year more responsibilities are placed on the teacher and less responsibilities are placed on students for their learning and comprehension." (teacher, 11–15 years experience)

"The more years that I work, the less effective I feel." (teacher, 16–20 years experience)

HIGH JOB SATISFACTION COMMENTS

"I absolutely love my job. I love watching the light bulb moments in children's eyes each day. It's easy to get bogged down in all the extras but at the end of the day, there's nothing else I'd rather do." (teacher, 6–10 years experience)

"It's what I was meant to do." (teacher, 26+ years experience)

"I believe my career has been meaningful and I've loved working with students." (teacher, 26+ years experience)

"I have always loved helping young kids learn." (teacher, 26+ years experience)

"I get such a sense of accomplishment and fullness from my job." (teacher, 6–10 years experience)

ATTITUDES TOWARD TECHNOLOGY

Another question in the survey asks if the respondent holds the attitude that technology in the classroom is detrimental or beneficial. A few comments from this question are as follows.

Selected the attitude that technology is detrimental in the classroom:

- "Students are on devices too long."

- "Our students are too dependent on technology to learn."

- "I wouldn't say technology is detrimental, but it's not satisfying when all you're doing is dealing with problems. Students damage devices, they have problems logging in, many struggle with password changes, and teachers have trouble with permission to download software and have to submit multiple tech support tickets."

Selected the attitude that technology is beneficial in the classroom:

- "I do not miss the bad old days because I adore how much progress is now possible, but I do miss just being able to teach. I lose 5–7 minutes of instruction time in my seventh hour class due to streaming to another campus, but I also love that those students have the option to take that class."

- "It makes my job easier."

- "I love using various programs and tools when they enhance and engage students' learning!"

- "Technology is a transformational tool in education."

There exists a wide range in the attitudes of teachers when it comes to whether technology is detrimental or beneficial for teaching and learning. Balancing the degree to which technology supports learning objectives takes time and experience with the tools provided.

Educators on Technology Integration

The following word cloud illustrates the results of asking respondents to select as many terms as apply to describe their view of technology integration. They were also provided with the option to add their own terms.

According to the responses, educators overwhelmingly agree that technology integration supports critical thinking, communication, collaboration, creativity, efficiency, and effectiveness, but they also describe it as overwhelming, frustrating, and somewhat confusing. Most have the mindset that technology integration is a supportive component to a classroom; therefore, those who support teachers with this endeavor have an obligation to do what they can to keep it exciting without adding to any associated negative feelings.

Take a moment to contribute to the Educator Well-Being Survey by sharing your perspective and opinions regarding technology integration. Scan the QR code provided to submit your responses. The data gathered through the survey will help others better understand what can be done to support you and other educators from around the world. Contributors may choose to remain anonymous.

  Educator Well-Being Survey
qr.page/g/1gdStSW1w5W

Self-Awareness

Being aware of one's own feelings and emotions is an important component of emotional well-being. This awareness can serve as a guidepost for understanding and behaving in beneficial ways. According to CASEL, with greater self-awareness, we can recognize our strengths and limitations and better understand ourselves in the ways shown in the diagram. Self-awareness is one of CASEL's five competencies and is a key step toward better emotional health (CASEL, 2023).

Benefits of Being Self-Aware

- Integrate personal and social identities
- Identify personal, cultural, and linguistic assets
- Identify one's emotions
- Demonstrate honesty and integrity
- Link feelings, values, and thoughts
- Examine prejudices and biases
- Experience self-efficacy
- Have a growth mindset
- Develop interests and a sense of purpose

CASEL offers a free course entitled An Introduction to Social and Emotional Learning designed to, "Learn more about social and emotional learning (SEL), reflect on how it connects to your daily life and your relationships with young people, and plan opportunities for SEL." The course includes application activities, a facilitation guide, and next steps. (CASEL, 2023)

To help one gain a greater sense of self as it pertains to one's emotional state and relates to their job, a variety of occupational psychological measurement tools are available.

CASEL's An Introduction to Social and Emotional Learning Course
qr.page/g/2dlUePQgqwo

THE LEICHTMAN BURNOUT SCALE

The Leichtman Burnout Scale is a tool based on dissertation research conducted by Kevin Leichtman that "seeks to provide a clear understanding of the burnout process specifically for educators." The scale is described in Edutopia's May 2022 article entitled "How Burned Out Are You? A Scale for Teachers," which identifies four levels of burnout and provides suggestions for teachers to identify their level of burnout as a step toward becoming more self-aware (Leichtman, 2022).

LEVEL 1: Passionate but Overwhelmed

Indicators:

- low feelings of self-efficacy
- negative coping strategies
- limited pursuit of passions

Suggestion: Employ positive, proactive coping mechanisms.

LEVEL 2: Overwhelmed and Becoming Cynical

Indicators:

- high levels of stress
- quick to become irritated (at work and home)
- bringing work home and not completing it
- feeling like there is never time for friends or family
- guilt from not doing enough for students

Suggestion: Seek support from a strong and positive mentor.

LEVEL 3: Cynical and Approaching Exhaustion

Indicators:

- isolation (in and out of work)
- feelings of paranoia (every school policy, program, etc., is out to get you and make your teaching day harder)
- a constant feeling that school goals and your goals will not be met
- a refusal to engage in professional development

Suggestion: Reduce role duties and seek mental health support.

LEVEL 4: Complete Exhaustion and Breakdown

Indicators:

- feelings of exhaustion every day (including holidays and summer)
- drastic increase in sick days/mental health days
- lack of optimism for career and personal life
- unusually frequent physical symptoms (colds/flus, stress-related illnesses, hospitalizations)

Suggestion: Take vital action. Prioritize and seek purpose.

 Edutopia's "How Burned Out Are You? A Scale for Teachers"
qr.page/g/jBEV1Uz18

MASLACH BURNOUT INVENTORY

The Maslach Burnout Inventory—Educators Survey (MBI-ES) by authors Christina Maslach, Susan E. Jackson, & Richard Schwab is a version of the original Maslach Burnout Inventory, which has been validated by extensive research since its publication in 1981. The survey addresses three different scales as follows:

1. Emotional exhaustion: measures feelings of being emotionally overextended and exhausted by one's work.

2. Depersonalization: measures an unfeeling and impersonal response toward recipients of one's instruction.

3. Personal accomplishment: measures feelings of competence and successful achievement in one's work.

   At the time of publication, the MBI-ES costs $50 and those who take it can receive an individual report for an additional $15.

Mind Garden's Maslach Burnout Inventory (MBI)
qr.page/g/30IMJgynFmX

JAWS JOB SATISFACTION SURVEY

The JAWS Job Satisfaction Survey has been developed to measure emotional reactions to one's job. It investigates peoples' affective responses to work stressors. The survey can be downloaded and self-scored under the condition that the results are shared for research purposes.

 Paul Spector's Job-Related Affective Well-being Scale JAWS
qr.page/g/3FLWkkfsVUW

MIND TOOLS

The Mind Tools website provides a wide variety of self-assessments to support emotional wellness at work which includes a Locus of Control Self-Assessment. With a free email registration, users can access videos, assessments, and articles. Additional resources are available as a paid subscription.

 Mind Tools Locus of Control Self-Assessment
qr.page/g/1rTk7PWvPh0

2.1 EVALUATE YOUR OWN JOB SATISFACTION

Before moving forward, take a moment to consider your own job satisfaction. As you were reading, did you recognize your experiences in any of the Leichtman Burnout Scale levels? Acknowledging feelings of satisfaction and dissatisfaction is a launching point for taking action, if needed.

The Importance of Self-Care

All too often, teachers put the needs of others over their own, sometimes to the detriment of their emotional well-being. And sometimes it seems the more one gives, the more that is taken. It is important that teachers commit to taking care of themselves. Self-care is the practice one takes to improve their mental and physical well-being. Self-care actions can be categorized as:

- physical actions: running, yoga, dancing, gardening, etc.

- sensory stimulation acts: listening to music, making art, eating, etc.

- emotional support experiences: seeking guidance from other teachers, family, friends, etc.

- spiritual experiences: prayer, meditation, attending church services, participating in retreats, etc.

- social experiences: book clubs, team sports, concerts, etc.

SELF-CARE IDEAS FOR EDUCATORS PADLET

Whether you have effective ideas or are looking for inspiration, visit this Self-Care for Educators Padlet to share and access a collection of ideas sorted by category. To share your own, select the category column and click the + to contribute. Add your idea as the heading of the post. You may provide your name or you may choose to remain anonymous.

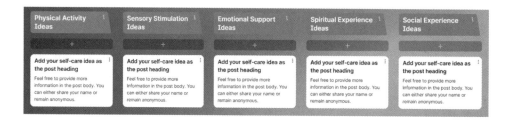

Tech for Teacher Wellness: Shared Self-Care Ideas Padlet
qr.page/g/5eTgsGLjpaL

2.2 PRACTICE SELF-CARE DAILY

As a promise to one's own emotional well-being, set a goal to practice a form of self-care daily if you are not already doing so. Use the ideas shared in the collaborative Self-Care Padlet if you need inspiration.

Mindfulness

According to *Psychology Today*, "Mindfulness encompasses two key ingredients: awareness and acceptance. Awareness is the knowledge and ability to focus attention on one's inner processes and experiences, such as the experience of the present moment. Acceptance is the ability to observe and accept—rather than judge or avoid—those streams of thought." (*Psychology Today* Staff, 2023). Practicing mindfulness can help put things in perspective and reduce anxiety. Being present and aware of our surroundings supports our emotional well-being. Mindfulness in education has primarily focused on its practice by students as an element of social-emotional learning, but practicing mindfulness can positively benefit the emotional well-being of teachers as well.

2.3 BECOME MORE MINDFUL

Being mindful and feeling present in the events of life has great value. When you find yourself in a moment of bliss, pause to pay attention to what you see, hear, feel, smell, and even taste. Recognizing the sensory inputs that bring you positive emotions will help you recall these details when you might need to call upon calming memories when feeling stressed or anxious.

Alternatively, if you find yourself feeling anxious or overwhelmed by growing to-do lists or experiencing a particularly stressful moment, try to ground yourself.

To ground oneself is to intentionally place your attention in the present moment. Grounding techniques are good to keep handy in your tool belt. Some people use tactile items like squishy balls or textured strips to divert their attention to their sense of touch. Another technique to ground oneself is to take a deep breath and notice what you see, hear, smell, taste, and feel. When the world seems to be spinning around us, taking a moment to be in the moment can help soothe an anxious mind.

Try Being Mindful

1. Deliberately and deeply breathe in and breathe out.
2. Concentrate on breathing.
3. While breathing, pay attention to your body.
4. Visualize any tension being released.

The Value of Deep Breathing

Intentional deep breaths slow down the body's physical response to stress, known as the fight-or-flight response. This is the body's way of preparing to react when it perceives physical threats. People under stress can develop threat physiological threat reactions to benign situations that aren't necessarily threatening. A student forgetting a password or having internet connectivity are issues that don't present actual threats to our livelihood; however, everyday classroom frustrations such as these can heighten our physiological responses. Over time, this repeated response causes elevated levels of the body's stress hormones and can exacerbate feelings of anxiety. Knowing how to slow down the body's response is a powerful tool to promote a greater sense of well-being and reduce feelings of stress.

Studies have shown the benefits of deep diaphragmatic breathing for dealing with feelings of stress and anxiety. One study in particular, *Effectiveness of Diaphragmatic Breathing for Reducing Physiological and Psychological Stress in Adults: A Quantitative Systematic Review*, sought to find out if the practice of deep breathing could be an effective alternative to pharmacological options. Researchers found that breathing deeply has a positive effect on lowering both physiological and psychological stress (Hopper et al., 2019).

Hopper's study includes data from a variety of studies that examine the impact of implementing the practice of deep breathing. Whether done each morning on the way to work, in between classes, or anytime you find yourself feeling stressed, diaphragmatic breathing is an effective way to minimize feelings of stress and anxiety. It takes little time to start a daily practice of deep breathing, and it does not take long to reap the benefits.

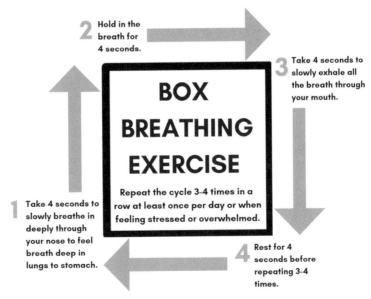

The box breathing strategy is an easy one to learn and can be relied upon to practice daily or when feeling anxious.

2.4 TAKE TIME & MAKE TIME FOR DAILY DEEP BREATHING

Right now, take a few moments to become familiar with this simple box breathing exercise. Then, consider when it can become a daily routine. It is something that can be practiced while driving to and from work or paired with daily tasks such as showering or dish washing.

Prioritize Your Own Well-Being

Consider this excerpt from M. Colleen Cruz's *Risk. Fail. Rise.: A Teacher's Guide to Learning from Mistakes:*

> "As teachers, we are caretakers by the nature of our positions. Our instinct almost always is to care for our students before we care for ourselves. This is a noble ideal. But it is also impossible. Children will always need more, so there is no clear end to the amount of giving a teacher can do. And when teachers give teaching their all, they often end up depleted, drained of the physical and emotional energy to be the sort of skilled practitioner we'd all like to be. Let me say that another way: when educators give so much to their students that they are feeling empty, they do not have the ability to do the sort of high-level thinking and creative work, let alone have the physical stamina to be the excellent teacher their children need. The heroic martyr teacher might make for great film, but it does not make for great instruction."

Teaching is as stressful as it is rewarding. To be of service to our students, teachers must take good care of themselves. If you are constantly feeling overwhelmed, stressed, or cynical, it is time to do something for yourself. *Mental Health America's Teachers: Protecting Your Mental Health* suggests the following to help protect your mental well-being (Mental Health America, 2023):

- Set boundaries and stick to them.
- Focus on the things within your control.
- Move your body.
- Stay in touch with friends and family.

- Keep up with self-care.
- Maintain reasonable expectations.

Support for Improved Well-Being

Self-care, mindfulness, and deep breathing all help, but they may not be enough to meet your emotional needs. There is a growing list of resources to help teachers as they explore feelings of burnout, isolation, and stress. To augment any local or regional options, the following list represents several available at the time this book is being written.

- Amber Harper, a kindergarten teacher and coach, supports teachers with her *Burned-In Teacher* podcast and resources and explores ways in which teachers can take steps toward improving burnout and life in general. Her book, *Hacking Teacher Burnout*, takes readers through steps to feel less isolated and more empowered (Harper, 2023). qr.page/g/1mEdxJtPH00

- *Education Support* has been providing support for teachers and school support personnel in the United Kingdom since 1877. They have mental wellness resources, training materials for school leaders, information about grant opportunities, and a hotline for immediate support. While some information available is public, other resources are exclusively for teachers in the U.K. qr.page/g/2QMpmY4x20R

- *Headspace for Educators* is a currently free resource for K–12 teachers in the United Kingdom, United States, Canada, and Australia. Educators can sign up for a free account to learn more about practicing mindfulness and to experience different guided activities for attaining balance, gaining focus, resetting, winding down, and many others. Users can adjust according to the amount of time they have, and many of the activities can take as little as three minutes (Headspace, 2023). qr.page/g/1CNlCfqTUeb

2.5 SEEK SUPPORT WHEN NEEDED WITHOUT HESITATION

At any point in your career, if you find yourself experiencing feelings of isolation, extreme cynicism, and complete burnout, it is imperative that you seek support. School leaders are beginning to recognize the need for emotional wellness support systems for teachers. Check with district leaders to inquire if any systems are in place for you to access. If none are available, reach out to a mental health counselor or contact a physician for guidance. HelpGuide.org provides a directory of international health helplines as well.

HelpGuide.org   Q Find Help Today

Mental Health   Health & Wellness   Children & Family   Relationships   Aging   Meditation

Directory of International Mental Health Helplines

Are you or someone you know in crisis? The following hotlines around the world can provide you with help.

Select your country: United States   UK   Ireland   Canada   Australia   New Zealand   India   Philippines   South Africa

Teacher Well-Being Impacts Students

In education, the recent focus has been on supporting the social-emotional health of students. While there is no denying the critical need to foster the social-emotional health of students, there is also a critical need to foster the social-emotional health of teachers. With consideration to the impact on student performance in mind, according to a 2021 study on the impact of teacher stress on student outcomes conducted by The University of Queensland in Brisbane, Australia, their results indicated that there are "... important downstream benefits for students" and "a broader value of stress-reduction and well-being programs for teachers" (Carroll et al., 2021).

Improvements to the emotional well-being of teachers will lead to greater job satisfaction and positively impact student outcomes—both emotionally and academically. While the tech strategies, suggestions, and resources provided in this book are not intended to be the panacea for all that ails teachers, it has been written with the purpose to be a practical guide for leveraging technology to foster one's overall well-being and promote career longevity.

Chapter 2 Reflections on Your Well-Being

Take a few moments to reflect and personalize the content provided in chapter 2.

- How would you describe your own level of self-awareness? Is it something you have considered or is this a new concept to you?

- Do you prioritize your own self-care?

- If so, how does it impact your sense of well-being?

- If not, what type seems to be a good fit for your lifestyle?

_____

_____

_____

_____

- Have you ever practiced mindfulness?

_____

_____

_____

_____

- If so, have you experienced any benefits from it?

_____

_____

_____

_____

- If not, how can you make time to do so?

_____

_____

_____

_____

- Have you ever practiced deep breathing exercises?

_____

_____

_____

_____

- If so, have you experienced any benefit from the practice?

- If not, how can you make time to start?

Practicing self-care, mindfulness, and deep breathing take intention and time to adopt as wellness habits. If you have not yet adopted any as habits, try adopting one at a time. Deep breathing exercises are easily integrated during the drive to or from work.

Share any reflections or thoughts that you feel comfortable sharing on social media with the hashtag #TeacherWellness to raise public awareness. Feel free to tag @realtechfored in your post.

Choose and Cultivate Seeds for Your Well-Being. Use this page to sketch about the strategies you'd like to sow. Consider your expectations for the growth you'll experience, the support and nurturing you'll need from coaches and school leaders; and illustrate how the strategies you choose to implement will positively impact your wellbeing.

Chapter 3

Boundaries

"I'm trying to find a better balance, but there's always so much to do or that I feel should be done. I create pressure for myself to do more at the suffering of my personal life."
—Heather, a Louisiana high school teacher with
16–20 years of experience in education

OVER THE YEARS, IT HAS BECOME EASIER FOR THE LINES BETWEEN WORK LIFE and home life to be erased. With digital communication, social media, and schoolwork available at our fingertips, work life can easily overwhelm home life. If you feel like your work–home balance is out of whack, it is time to consider the importance of boundaries.

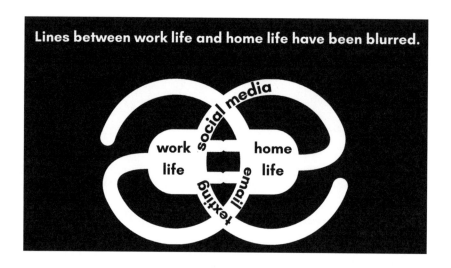

Establishing healthy boundaries and sticking to them is a foundational element in emotional well-being. While setting boundaries early in one's career is most beneficial, too often teachers find their work lives intruding on their home lives more and more as the years pass, so it is important to understand that boundaries can be established at any time.

A 2018 PositivePsychology.com article by J. Nash entitled "How to Set Healthy Boundaries and Build Positive Relationships" shares some tips regarding work boundaries, which have been adapted and contextualized for teachers as follows:

- *Assess your personal needs first.* This requires some introspection and development of self-awareness as discussed in the previous chapter.

- *Communicate your boundaries professionally and clearly.* Strategies for doing so will be provided in forthcoming chapters.

- *Establish working hours.* As a teacher, consider setting a limited amount of time outside of the workday to attend to email, office hours, and other duties.

- *Delegate your workload.* Teachers can take advantage of certain tech features to assist with this. These will be described later in chapter 5.

- *Be okay with saying no.* This is hard for some teachers. Really hard. But it can and should be done to avoid becoming overwhelmed with duties outside of the classroom.

- *Take time off.* As best as possible, try to leave work at work. Teachers are lifelong learners and often embrace professional development over summer. While it may be work-related, participating in enrichment learning opportunities can be valuable as long as one does not do so when overwhelmed. Rest is important.

- *Use technology to establish boundaries.* Several strategies will be shared in this chapter to help.

Boundaries Are Necessary

Educational technology makes a positive impact on teaching and learning every single day. Teachers use tech to:

- communicate more effectively
- provide every student with the opportunity for personalized formative feedback
- differentiate learning experiences to meet the needs of their students
- make learning accessible to all learners
- make the daily work of teaching more efficient

While edtech has many advantages, it is vital that the ability to access and connect 24-7 is contained to maintain a healthy and reasonable work and personal life balance. According to the results shared in the Educator Well-Being survey, more than 60% of respondents reported that their work life inhibits their personal life.

The Edutopia article "Defending a Teacher's Right to Disconnect" by Youki Terada provides additional context. "Technology is rapidly pushing things toward a breaking point. The proliferation of computers, and especially cell phones, is putting the last vestiges of personal space at risk, compelling teachers to spend more time outside of school hours planning tech-enriched lessons while responding to nighttime emails and text messages. This pattern of incursion—researchers call it 'techno-invasion' or 'pervasive connectivity'—can make them feel as though they're on call at all hours of the day and even late into the night." (Terada, 2021)

This chapter focuses on practical strategies for establishing these boundaries and includes concrete examples for doing so. Some of the examples are simple with minimal impact when integrated in isolation. However, when all suggestions are put into practice, they will work together to help you establish a healthier balance between your work and personal lives for a meaningful positive impact.

3.1 GUARD YOUR PERSONAL PHONE NUMBER

We have all done it. While supporting our students and work-related matters are important, it is just as important to remain aware that using a personal device to make a work phone call or text to a parent/guardian can exponentially increase access to you and your personal time. Providing access to your personal phone number may feel helpful at the time, but doing so will have significant implications. Keep your personal contact information private to establish boundaries, maintain a sense of professionalism, and for personal safety.

Consider the act of sharing your personal phone number as an open invitation that never expires. In the beginning of one's career, it may not be an issue. But over the course of five, ten, or fifteen years, it will become exhausting. Therefore, it is important to get into the habit of reaching out to parents or guardians consistently via school email, with a school phone, or through a messaging service like Remind (remind.com), which protects your personal information. If your number is already circulating in the "parentsphere," here are some simple suggestions moving forward.

3.2 REDIRECT, IDENTIFY, AND BLOCK

Some folks will respect your time; other folks will take advantage of having access to you and not consider your personal time; and still other folks (you know who they are) have no qualms about sharing your number with other parents or even with students. When contacted on your personal device, adopt a policy of "redirect, identify, and block."

When you get a message from anyone regarding work issues, first *redirect* them to your work email. Then, if you do not already have the number in your contacts, *identify* who they are when they send the email to your school account and add them to your contacts so you can screen any subsequent messages.

When Contacted on Your Personal Phone...

REDIRECT
Reply with a statement like, "I am unable to assist you at this time, please contact me at my work email address and I'll get back to you as soon as possible. Thank you!

IDENTIFY
As soon as you identify who the person is, add them to your phone contacts so you know who they are for screening purposes.

BLOCK
If they contact you on your personal device again, redirect them, then block their number.

NOTE: As tempting as it may be to give them a reply or an answer to their question, in order to establish healthy boundaries, it is important that you refrain from doing so.

If they contact you on your personal number again, *block* them. And do not feel guilty for doing so. Imagine if every professional in every other career provided their clients, patients, or customers with personal access 24-7. Your personal time is valuable and needs to be focused on personal matters.

3.3 SEPARATE WORK EMAIL FROM PERSONAL EMAIL

Having convenient access to email is a modern necessity. However, intermingling one's personal and work email should be avoided to minimize access. If your mobile device provides the feature to add your work email to be threaded with your personal email, remove your work email address and install the appropriate app (Outlook, Gmail, etc.) for separate access. This keeps your personal email thread separated from your work email thread. An even better idea is to remove your work email altogether from your personal device. This forces you to access another device to check your work email.

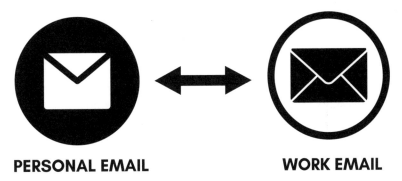

Email Management

Everyone has their own email management needs, and several suggestions provided later in this book are intended to help minimize the time it takes to attend to email. For some, checking email outside of work hours makes better use of the hours spent in the classroom. If your needs require that you are attentive to email outside of your school day, then establish a *reasonable* schedule for doing so and stick to it.

Perhaps you designate an extra fifteen minutes of time either before or after school three times a week as your email response time. Maybe you would rather attend to it on Tuesday and Thursday evenings for an extra thirty minutes each night. The purpose of a schedule is to help establish boundaries and give you the opportunity to provide email response expectations as described in the next strategy, which will help alleviate some of the stress associated with day-to-day email responsibilities.

ESTABLISH A REASONABLE EMAIL SCHEDULE

15 minutes in AM before school & 15 minutes in PM after school

Adjust as necessary to prevent from having to attend to work email at all on the weekends. May need to adjust as email volume increase or decreases throughout the year.

3.4 ESTABLISH EMAIL RESPONSE EXPECTATIONS

Some teachers have no stress related to email, while others feel a sense of urgency, even anxiety, when they check their email inboxes. If you are in the latter group, proactively providing email expectations will minimize those feelings which contribute to anxiety, stress, and burnout.

The time it takes to address email varies greatly by individual. Some teachers have more students than others, which can result in a higher volume of emails. Some teachers serve on multiple administrative committees, which communicate via email. Some teachers are sponsors of clubs, and others sponsor multiple school organizations. Email habits are also varied. Some teachers feel compelled to keep their inbox notifications at zero, while others have no issue with an ever-increasing total. Some teachers make a habit to check email before their day starts and at the end of the day, and some teachers decide to spend time outside of the classroom to tend to email messages.

No matter what your email obligations and habits may be, establishing a schedule as mentioned in the previous strategy is beneficial. By doing so, you set clear boundaries by which to abide. Once you determine what sort of routine is best suited to your email needs, consider how to communicate this routine to provide reasonable expectations to those who send you messages. Expectations can be stated as: "Email responses can be expected within 48–72 hours," or as "Emails received after 4:00 p.m. Monday–Thursday will be read the following day. Emails received after 4:00 p.m. on a Friday will be read on the following Monday."

Meredith Boullion

 meredith.boullion@gmail.com

 @realtechfored

 meredith-masar-boullion-70899b9b

While email is checked daily, expect a response within 36–48 hours.

Add email response expectations that align to your established email schedule to your email signature image.

Take the time to consider this strategy and draft a message that best aligns to your needs. What other information would be useful to share? Once you develop an email response expectation message, communicate it as often and in as many places as is possible. Doing so eliminates the sense of urgency some may feel when it comes to addressing email outside of work hours. It gives you a mental buffer and prevents those who email you from having unrealistic expectations about when they will receive a response from you.

Instructions for Creating Custom Email Signatures

To create an email signature, you can keep it simple and stick to the text editing tools provided in your email, or you can use a tool like Canva, Adobe Express, PowerPoint, or any other you may prefer to create a signature card with graphics. Before you follow the steps to create custom email signatures, you'll want to have any graphic already made and saved as an image that's easily accessible.

Steps to Create a Gmail Signature from a Desktop:

1. Open **Gmail**.

2. In the top right, click *Settings > See All Settings*.

3. Scroll down to the *Signature* section and click + *Create New*.

4. Inside the text editor, add the information you would like to share in your email response notifications. Add any image(s) you may have created or would like to use by clicking the image icon.

5. Scroll down to select *Save Changes*.

6. Send a test email to yourself to make sure it appears as intended.

 Create a Gmail signature
qr.page/g/3uPQFbZ4TqT

Instructions for setting up a Gmail signature while using an Android or iOS device can be accessed with the QR code or short URL.

Steps to Create an Outlook on the Web Signature

1. Open **Outlook on the web** through Microsoft 365.

2. In the top right, click the gear icon for *Settings > View All Outlook settings*.

3. Select *Compose and reply* and click *+ New Signature*.

4. Inside the text editor, add what information you would like to share in your email response notifications. Add any image(s) you may have created or would like to use by clicking the image icon.

5. Click *Save*.

6. Send a test email to yourself to make sure it appears as intended.

Note: Instructions for setting up an Outlook desktop app signature can be accessed with the QR code.

 Create and add a signature to messages in Outlook
qr.page/g/wmxbkY5wAL

3.5 LEVERAGE AUTOMATED EMAIL RESPONSE FEATURES

Generating an automated vacation or out-of-office response sends an automatic reply to those who email you when you schedule it to do so. This feature is intended to be used when one cannot respond to email due to being out of the office, but it can be leveraged to communicate information automatically during the instructional day. Consider what information would be most beneficial for you to send as an automated response.

Hello,
While I check email regularly throughout the day, my office hours are from 7:15AM-
7:30AM and 3:00PM-3:30PM Monday-Friday. If you are a parent/guardian with general
questions, please visit my <u>teacher website</u> for responses to frequently asked questions.
If you find the answer to your emailed question, please let me know so I can mark your
message as resolved. If you are a parent/guardian with concerns not addressed on my
website, you can expect a response within 24-72 hours.
Thank You,
Mrs. Boullion

Instructions for Automated Email Responses

Gmail: Out-of-Office or Vacation Reply

1. Open Gmail in Chrome on a desktop.

2. In the top right, click *Settings > See all settings*.

3. Scroll down to find *Vacation responder*.

4. Select the dates for when you would like the automated responses to
   begin and end.

5. Select whether your response is sent to everyone, only your contacts, or
   only people in your organization.

6. Add a subject to the message.

Note: Instructions for setting up on Android or iOS devices are available through
the QR code/short URL.

 Create a vacation reply for Gmail
qr.page/g/4QpV6yuUaX6

Outlook: Automated Out-of-Office Replies

1. Open Outlook on the web through a desktop browser.

2. In the top right, click the gear icon for *Settings > View all Outlook settings*.

3. Select *Automatic replies*.

4. Toggle the button to *Turn automatic replies on.*

5. You may opt to set up a range of dates and times for them to occur.

6. To keep the automated message from being sent to those who email you from within your organization (other teachers, administrators, etc.), scroll to select *Send replies outside your organization.*

7. Add your drafted message in the text box. Here, you can insert the link to your teacher website, grade center, or any other resource that may provide responses to your most frequently asked email questions.

8. Click *Save.*

Note: Instructions for setting up automatic out-of-office replies for the desktop app can be accessed with the QR code/short URL.

Send automatic (out of office) replies in Outlook
qr.page/g/OyrP7yuflD

3.6 MINIMIZE THE DINGS AND ZINGS OF CONSTANT NOTIFICATIONS

While some reminders are useful and important, a multitude of constant notifications becomes a stressor. Do you really need to know every time a student submits an assignment? Probably not, but it is important to be reminded of an after-school conference or faculty meeting.

It can take some time to go into all the programs used in a day to adjust the notification settings, but it is possible. A Google search can typically guide you through the process. But if the task of digging into the settings of your LMS, email application, and any other source of notifications is too daunting, consider taking advantage of digital wellness features provided by the same tech companies who just a few years ago worked so hard to get everyone to pay attention to them.

Do Not Disturb and *Focus* features are available when using Windows, Apple, and Android devices. Apple users can create and schedule a custom Focus with iOS 15 and iPadOS 15 or later, and Android users can use Digital Wellbeing. Apple, Android, and Windows each provide users with the ability to set the device to not be disturbed.

Table 3-1: Digital Do Not Disturb and Digital Wellbeing Features

Tool	Description	QR Code
Android Digital Wellbeing	Provides Android users with features and controls to disconnect digitally at times set by the user.	qr.page/g/33baStiqWxU
Android Do Not Disturb	Provides Android users with the ability to temporarily set the device to not be disturbed.	qr.page/g/4koITQzgoE4

Tool	Description	QR Code
Apple Focus	Provides iPhone and iPad users with iOS 15 or later with tools to set up focus times to digitally disconnect.	qr.page/g/4es3LARMxPS
Apple Do Not Disturb	Provides iOS users with the ability to temporarily set the device to not be disturbed.	qr.page/g/2OhCGDHcUVl
Windows Focus Assist	Provides Windows users with the ability to set the device to not be disturbed.	qr.page/g/5rKNJ12KS01

Considered in isolation, the suggestions in this chapter may seem like they will have minimal impact, but the compounded effect of integrating all of them will yield results over time. Whether you are just beginning your career or are well-established, taking steps within your control to firmly establish boundaries and positively impact the balance between your work and personal lives is a step toward better emotional well-being.

Chapter 3 Reflections on Boundaries

Take a moment to consider any of the following items presented in this chapter.

- Is your work email currently threaded with your personal email?

    _____

    _____

    _____

    _____

- If so, take a moment to install the email app used for work and remove your work email from your personal thread OR remove access to your work email from your phone completely.

    _____

    _____

    _____

    _____

- Do you have a reasonable schedule for attending to your work email?

    _____

    _____

    _____

    _____

- If not, take a moment to consider what one would look like for you.

    _____

    _____

    _____

    _____

- Are you familiar with any focus or do not disturb features on your work and home devices?

  _____

  _____

  _____

  _____

- If not, take time to learn about these features and utilize them for your own benefit.

  _____

  _____

  _____

  _____

Establishing boundaries is easier for some than for others. If doing so feels like you are doing a disservice to others, keep this quote from Brené Brown in mind: "Daring to set boundaries is about having the courage to love ourselves even when we risk disappointing others."

Share other suggestions you have for establishing boundaries that you feel comfortable sharing on social media with the hashtag #TeacherWellness to raise public awareness. Feel free to tag @realtechfored as well.

Choose and Cultivate Seeds for Establishing Your Boundaries. Use this page to sketch about the strategies you'd like to sow. Consider your expectations for the growth you'll experience, the support and nurturing you'll need from coaches and school leaders; and illustrate how the strategies you choose to implement will positively impact your wellbeing.

Chapter 4

Foster and Promote
Digital Positivity

"Realize the impact you will make on future generations. . . . You will be convinced that you have chosen a profession that gives your life a purpose."
—Suresh, a Louisiana teacher and curriculum coach
with 21–26 years of experience as an educator

TECHNOLOGY HAS THE INCREDIBLE CAPACITY TO POSITIVELY IMPACT OTHERS like never before. We share ideas on social media, connecting and learning from other educators from all around the world. An amazing characteristic about educators is our enthusiasm to share what works. Sharing effective practices and beneficial resources is an act of generosity to not just benefit other teachers, but to help teachers do what is best for students. Social media platforms used to support teaching and learning can become generally beneficial and impactful spaces for teachers.

Managing Social Media

On occasion, enthusiasm for sharing on public platforms can create problems for teachers. For example, someone might get caught up in the moment and forget to respect the privacy of their students by sharing student images in their personal social media posts. Or perhaps, while in a heightened emotional state, they might vent over something that happened in the classroom to seek emotional support. In either situation, they open themselves up to public scrutiny and must face potential consequences of their actions no matter how benign their intentions were. Sometimes, it can even put their reputation and career at risk.

In a public world, it is important for educators to be ever mindful when using social media platforms to connect and share. Oversharing details and circumstances encountered in the classroom can create regret that leads to emotional turmoil. This chapter provides strategies to foster and promote digital positivity.

4.1 ALWAYS KNOW YOUR AUDIENCE

Sharing information with people in real life is different from sharing with people through social media. For one's best interests to be served, it is important to always know your audience. This is true when writing an essay or speech and remains so when posting on on any social media platform. When writing a school essay, there is an audience of one (the instructor) who provides feedback and points out any errors with your best interest in mind to help elevate the quality of your content. Social media differs in that one post could reach an audience of hundreds or even thousands. Some readers will quickly and eagerly comment to point out any errors, whereas others may try to start an argument out of boredom or resentment, and still others quietly judge you from behind their screens. In other words, not every person in your social media circle has your best interest in heart. Therefore, it is important to always know your audience. Here are a few best practices for doing so.

- Avoid accepting friend or follow requests from people you do not know in real life, or at least from those whose identities you cannot confirm.

- If you get a request from someone you thought was already in your audience, it may be fraudulent. Before accepting the request, reach out to your friend and confirm it is legitimate. Their account may have been compromised, so it could be important that they are aware of the request.

- Periodically review your audience and seriously contemplate removing those with whom you have no contact. Just like in real life, it is not about the number of friends or followers you have; it is about the quality of the relationships.

- Check your platform settings to ensure your posts are reaching your intended audience. Are your posts set to be public or private? Can what you share to your friends or followers in turn be shared by them with others? Can others tag you in photos or posts?

If you are or intend to become a social media influencer, then these suggestions may not be for you. However, being more cognizant of your audience is a preventative measure to maintain your privacy and prevent others from potentially damaging your reputation or perhaps inflicting emotional turmoil.

4-1 Table: Review and Adjust Your Social Media Privacy Settings

Platform	QR Code	Short URL
Facebook		qr.page/g/2pyD3jPIJag
Instagram		qr.page/g/1KkG5CkoSJF
TikTok		qr.page/g/392rDDGZO4V

Platform	QR Code	Short URL
X		qr.page/g/50QkKyr34sB
YouTube		qr.page/g/36aqo8DDxgJ

While specific websites for the resources referenced are provided with URLs and QR codes, digital locations for information changes frequently. Therefore, a Teacher Resources section is provided at the end of the book with more general URLs for the resources should the websites have any changes.

4.2 UNDERSTAND AND AVOID THE ALGORITHM OF NEGATIVITY

After considering your audience, the next consideration is to evaluate the content that you are consuming. Social media sites use sophisticated methods for gathering data from their users. Spending a nanosecond longer reading negative posts or interacting with content that makes one feel worse rather than better can eventually result in an unintentional cascade of negativity that we inadvertently caused.

Algorithms are used to customize user experiences. They are beneficial when they help us locate relevant content based on our recent interactions and searches. However, algorithms can also become detrimental to one's emotional health.

Imagine two people who set up accounts on a new social media platform at the same time. They ensure their settings are alike, and for all intents and purposes, they establish identical profiles in an attempt to mask any differences that may be detected regarding age, demographics, race, ideology, etc. As new users, they both encounter the same content as they scroll through the feed of information. Then, Person 1 decides to interact with content considered pessimistic in nature, while Person 2 interacts with content considered to be more optimistic. With user algorithms in place, it will not take long for the two users to report different scrolling experiences while using the social network. This is even the case with a Google search (though not in dark or private mode, which provides some anonymity).

Different scrolling experiences will elicit different sets of emotions in the users. While Person 2, who engaged with more positive content, feels no negative change in mood after scrolling, Person 1 may soon find themself doomscrolling without intentionally doing so. Doomscrolling is the act of continuing to scroll through negative content or bad news which leads to feelings of negativity, anxiety, and stress. Many people have no idea they are feeling this way due to the algorithms that are in place. It's like swimming a little off from others, then being swept into a whirlpool and left to drown. It is important to keep the power of algorithm in mind to prevent a spiral into negativity from happening. One is influenced by what one consumes.

An October 2022 study, "Doomscrolling Scale: Its Association with Personality Traits, Psychological Distress, Social Media Use, and Well-Being," finds evidence regarding the ill effects of doomscrolling on our mental wellness. Through a variety of measures, the team found that "doomscrolling was significantly and negatively related to life satisfaction, . . . mental well-being, . . . harmony in life, . . . and positively related to psychological distress . . ." (Satici et al., 2022).

If you find yourself consuming negative content that intensifies your negative emotions, there are ways to avoid it. R. Blank, founder of the site Healthier Tech, shares advice for protecting your well-being in a Healthier Tech blog post entitled "Do Social Media Algorithms Favor Content That Affects Your Well-being?" Blank states:

> The first thing you can do to prevent social media from interfering with your well-being is to make your feed a place where you can consume positive content. You can do that by following accounts that post positive and wholesome content. And at the same time, unfollow any user or account that makes you feel bad about yourself or the world at large. Besides that, you can also anonymously report negative content and content that spreads hate and misinformation. After some time of doing this, you'll have let social media algorithms know that positive content is what you like. And they will start showing you the same (Blank, 2023).

Algorithms in Action

Try this next time you're with a friend: enter identical search terms in Edge, Google, or Safari. Scroll through the results to see how different they may be. Can you tell how the algorithms read you both differently?

4.3 ADJUST SOCIAL MEDIA FOR EMOTIONAL WELL-BEING

When you find yourself scrolling through your social media feeds, ignore the temptation to interact with posts that skew negative. Sometimes, depending on one's frame of mind, it can be difficult. If it looks like clickbait or content designed to elicit strong emotions of anger or fear, avoid it. If you find your scrolling experience to be more negative than positive, use the features provided by social media companies to control what is shown in your feeds.

4-2 Table: Social Media Feed Management

Platform	QR Code to Instructions	Short URL to Instructions
Facebook		qr.page/g/42AScWMJyIk
Instagram		qr.page/g/15a6mS7Ddpd

Platform	QR Code to Instructions	Short URL to Instructions
TikTok		qr.page/g/113KZCCy05c
X		qr.page/g/4wphjyT6NkG
YouTube		qr.page/g/4iZAlT1JmjR

While specific websites for the resources referenced are provided with URLs and QR codes, digital locations for information changes frequently. Therefore, a Teacher Resources section is provided at the end of the book with more general URLs for the resources should the websites have any changes.

4.4 TAP INTO THE POWER OF POSITIVITY

Technology that is used to connect teachers from around the world and to enable them to share best practices is potentially one of the most transformational uses of technology in education. No longer are we teaching in isolation, and great ideas often spread like wildfire. There is no better time than now to find inspiration and support as a teacher. And right now, teachers need all the inspiration and support they can find.

Jennifer Gonzalez, author of the Cult of Pedagogy blog, proposed the idea of finding "marigolds" in her 2013 post entitled "Find Your Marigold: The One Essential Rule for New Teachers." In it, she provides advice for new teachers with a simple rule: "Surround yourself with good people" (Gonzalez, 2013). This rule should be followed by all teachers, whether you are a new or more experienced teacher, throughout your career. The notion of finding marigolds should also be extended into the digital world.

Whether or not you participate in social media, many options are available for finding beneficial educator content through technology. Digital marigolds can be found sharing beneficial information through blogs, email newsletters, websites, or podcasts—much like my favorite marigold, Jennifer herself. The key is to find these marigolds in the digital world and visit them when you find yourself in need of inspiration or support.

Social media profiles and groups can also provide a way to positively impact your professional learning network (PLN). X, the platform formerly known as Twitter, has traditionally been a popular platform for educators, with scheduled X chats to share information and resources. Private Facebook groups are available to join and communicate and collaborate with others in your grade level or specialty area. The creation of new social media platforms will continue to provide the chance for educators to connect. While the popularity and trust in sites may wax and wane, you can be assured that no matter the medium, educators will find a way to make the most of their ability to connect and share.

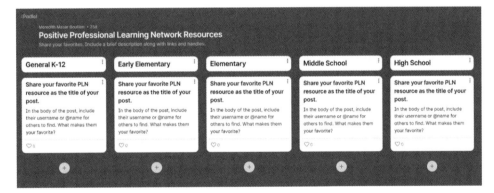

Who are the positive influences in your PLN?

Take this opportunity to share a favorite resource from your own PLN in a Padlet organized by grade level. Let others know how to find them on the platform (handles or links) and what makes them a favorite for you.

 Positive Professional Learning Network Resources Padlet
qr.page/g/ZWNsoUJWlq

Misty Savario (@mistykrazyteach), a first-grade ISTE-certified educator shares advice for using social media to expand one's PLN. "My advice for teachers is to find like-minded teachers who you can collaborate with and learn from. It can also be helpful to follow teacher products and companies to learn tips and tricks on how to use their resources. Using social media has helped me collaborate with teachers as pen pals, and I have made teacher friends all over the world. It has also given me the opportunity to try new tech products with my students."

4.5 RECOGNIZE GROWTH WITH GRATITUDE

All too often, our energy is focused on the things that we can improve. As educators, it is in our nature to nurture growth. Inherently, in the effort to help others grow, we address the things that we see that may need improvement in our students: reading fluency, problem-solving ability, athletic prowess, social skills, or self-management. Sometimes, it is a challenge to see the growth beyond a critical eye.

Growth deserves attention. Seeing student progress is the realization of all the work done by you and the student. When you make strides in the classroom, take a moment to fully appreciate it and feel gratitude. If it feels like a long time since you felt gratitude in the classroom, make a concerted effort to use fresh eyes to be a witness to the growth. Whether the growth is due to your efforts or the efforts of another, share your appreciation with a quick email to the student, their parents/guardians, or even a co-worker whose efforts you notice and appreciate. Feeling gratitude and expressing it toward others nourishes and flourishes an environment of well-being.

4.6 CULTIVATE DIGITAL KINDNESS

The social-emotional connections made in a classroom are more important than ever to our students. A kind classroom benefits the well-being of all. Teachers have an opportunity to cultivate a climate of kindness in the real world as well as in the digital world. One way to do so digitally is to create a simple Google or Microsoft Form where students can submit compliments for one another. Share the form by creating a QR code to post in the classroom or link on your teacher website. Results can be screened (especially advisable in middle school), then sorted by students to ensure everyone has some to their name. Then, their results can be shared as an end-of-the-year gift or to each student through email. Many teachers already incorporate this type of bucket-filling activity on paper, which may be all that is needed.

Teachers can create a way for students and teachers to share encouraging words. This option is an easier choice for teachers with large numbers of students. Tools like Padlet and Flip are great options for this sort of activity, which cultivates a climate of kindness and builds a sense of community in the classroom. Activities such as this support **ISTE Standard for Educators 2.3.a**, which suggests that educators "create experiences for learners to make positive, socially responsible contributions and exhibit empathetic behavior online that build relationships and community."

Interactive Experience

Experience an example of this type of activity yourself by contributing to the Padlet any words of wisdom or inspiring advice that have helped you get through tough times in the classroom. *Note: If you opt to use Padlet in your classroom for a similar sort of activity, go into the settings and ensure that it is set for you to approve posts before they go live. The same feature is also available if using Flip and is highly encouraged to keep things appropriate and positive.*

Tech for Teacher Wellness: Share Your Wisdom and Inspiration
qr.page/g/3zWMDnBCkc9

Chapter 4 Reflections on Positivity

Take some time to reflect upon and follow any of the suggestions provided in chapter 4 that might be effective for keeping your mindset positive.

- If you are a social media user, take the time to go through your friends list and followers. What may have seemed like a legitimate account a few years ago might look phony or phishy today.

  _____
  _____
  _____
  _____

- For any social media profile you regularly use, check out your privacy settings. Ensure you have them set for your own best interests. This is a good practice to do any time there are major operating system or app updates.

  _____
  _____
  _____
  _____

- Remain mindful of algorithms and share this info with as many people as will listen. When facing an epidemic of anxiety, every little thing we can do to preserve our emotional wellness needs to be done, and those methods shared.

  _____
  _____
  _____
  _____

- When you read about getting caught in the whirlpool of negativity, did anyone or anything come to mind? Take a few moments to purge your feeds and adjust them for a better scrolling experience.

_____

_____

_____

_____

When social media elicits more negative feelings than positive ones, it is perfectly acceptable to take a break. In fact, taking time away from social media from time to time can help one's overall sense of well-being.

Right now, take a few moments to send a shout-out email, text, or @mention to someone who has been a positive influence in your teaching life to express your gratitude.

Choose and Cultivate Seeds for Positivity. Use this page to sketch about the strategies you'd like to sow. Consider your expectations for the growth you'll experience, the support and nurturing you'll need from coaches and school leaders; and illustrate how the strategies you choose to implement will positively impact your wellbeing.

Author's Note

At this point in the book, readers have been given a wide variety of seeds to consider sowing to:

- improve one's sense of well-being
- develop reasonable boundaries for a better work/home life balance
- promote digital positivity to foster a healthier mindset

It is important to understand that even if you adopt all of suggestions provided thus far, you should not expect a change in your well-being to happen immediately. Making changes to positively impact one's well-being takes time.

If you are currently experiencing feelings of being overwhelmed, I suggest you pause and bookmark this page to return to later. The following chapter contains strategies for leveraging edtech features to make a teacher's workday more efficient, and it provides a multitude of resources from which to choose, which is a lot of information to process.

Once you are ready to proceed, approach chapter 5 with the consideration that while the strategies may be effective for you, it may be best to select only one tool that is readily available for use in your classroom, preferably one with which you may already be familiar. By no means are *all* the resources shared meant to be learned and integrated. The suggestions provided have been reliable throughout the years, many of which are available in school districts around the world.

Chapter 5

Efficiency

"Technology makes my life and my students' lives easier."
—Miranda, a Louisiana curriculum coach
with 6–10 years of experience as an educator)

ONE OF THE MOST INCREDIBLE FEATURES OF EDTECH IS THE ABILITY TO become more efficient in the classroom and free up precious time throughout the workday, minimizing the time you might spend on work tasks while at home. Perhaps you already take advantage of some of the strategies in this chapter. But maybe you have not known how to do so, have not had the time to invest in learning these strategies, or have not had a chance to implement them.

As stated in the author's note at the end of the previous chapter, the resources described in this chapter are common edtech tools that are available in schools. I would suggest that the strategies be integrated using the tools with which you are most familiar, minimizing potential frustration and technostress. If you feel frustrated or stressed when attempting to integrate the tool to support the strategy, take a break, do a few rounds of box breathing, and revisit the chapter at a later time.

5.1 AUTOMATE EMAIL

Attending to email is a time-consuming process. To make it less so, chapter 3 suggests that you establish response expectations and address commonly asked questions by linking to your teacher website in your signature and in an automated reply. Another strategy to lessen the toll of email is to take advantage of productivity features found in Gmail and Outlook.

Both Gmail and Outlook enable the user to create folders for a more organized inbox. Both services also provide a way to sort email messages for you. The key for success with this strategy is to establish rules for a sorting system according to your needs and to reevaluate those needs periodically. For example, setting up a rule so that another teacher's email goes directly into a folder named *To Ignore* one year could become problematic should that person become an administrator or change roles the following year.

The two services differ in the features they offer and in how automation is set up, but they both provide the ability to automate and triage messages that appear in your inbox. This gives you the chance to attend to the messages that need more immediate attention versus those that can wait. A little time investment setting up email automation can reduce the stress you may feel when checking email throughout the school day.

5-1 Table: Setting Up Email Automation

Platform	Available Features	QR Code
Gmail	Create and use folders and labels to organize Create rules to filter email Split emails using priority inbox	qr.page/g/31Xpjb49Ouq
Outlook on the web	Create and use folders and categories to organize Customize rules to send messages to folders to declutter inbox Right-click on the message to use the snooze feature to address the message at a later date and time—takes no set-up	qr.page/g/10DbV92B4hv

5.2 FAQ RESPONSES AS AUTOMATED REPLIES

The last strategy provided a way to leverage the features of automated responses. Consider how many emails could have been avoided had the information the sender sought been immediately addressed. Taking a proactive step to include FAQs and answers in an out-of-office or vacation reply can provide emailed inquiries with immediate solutions to access independently. Here are a few topics that can be addressed with this strategy.

- general grading information, procedures, and expectations
- how to access your website
- directions for enrolling in or signing up your school notification system like Remind
- directions to find student instructional resources

If you find yourself repeatedly responding to emailed questions asking about the same topics, this strategy can help you. A key to success with this strategy is to include a statement in bold print that says something like, "***If you find a solution to your email in these FAQs before I have the chance to reply, kindly let me know so I can mark your email inquiry as resolved. This gives me more time for my students. Thank you.***"

The more proactive you are with providing responses and solutions to the most frequently asked questions received by email, the less time you will have to spend responding, which will reduce your email workload. Think of this strategy as building the self-sufficiency of parents and guardians. People are accustomed to having access to what they need when they need it. It is a win-win strategy.

5.3 COMMUNICATE STUDENT EXPECTATIONS EFFECTIVELY

Parents and guardians need to know what students are expected to complete to be successful in your class. Having the information communicated clearly and in a way that is easily accessible can be a proactive approach to minimize email questions.

When possible, streamline the digital communication process for efficiency. Here are some suggestions for evaluating the tools being used to determine if it is a possibility.

- If you use a messaging service like Remind, visit the appropriate service's support site to see if the LMS or website host currently being used by your school or district supports the ability to embed messages. Embedding messages sent via a messaging service on your website keeps you from having to update the same information in multiple locations.

- If you use an LMS for multiple courses, visit their support site to determine if they provide the ability to broadcast announcements to multiple courses or if there is the ability to embed their integrated announcements or calendar tools on websites.

- Accessing edtech support resources has become more user-friendly. A good suggestion is to bookmark any support sites for programs being used or to any district resources provided for edtech support.

- To learn what features might be available to make the communication process more efficient, search the appropriate support sites for terms like "shared calendars" or "embedding announcements on public sites."

It can be a huge time saver to keep the number of places a teacher needs to update announcements on to a minimum. If you don't have access to a public website, the ability to broadcast information across an LMS, or a feature to update information in multiple places, there are still several options for creating a public teacher website that have the ability to include embedded content to streamline the communication process, as described in the next strategy.

5.4 MAINTAIN A PUBLIC TEACHER WEBSITE

School websites and LMS programs offer different levels of guest or public access. Some districts may only provide user accounts for students, limiting the ease with which class information is shared with parents and guardians, while other districts may provide and manage parent and guardian guest access. If you are unsure about this, inquire with your district to ensure you are following protocols and expectations.

If you already have access to a public site that can communicate information, this strategy may not be useful and may be extraneous. However, if public access to class information is limited, there are free options for creating a website to use and share. The world—teachers, students, parents, and guardians included—has become accustomed to access to resources on-demand. A self-serve teacher website might include:

- embedded announcements, weekly agendas, forms, class policies and procedures, and videos to support at-home tasks to prevent the need to update in multiple locations

- units at a glance

- required class materials

- read-only shared links to student resources including folders where content or information is housed

- early finisher websites links

- testing support resource links

- tutoring services resources links

- office hours

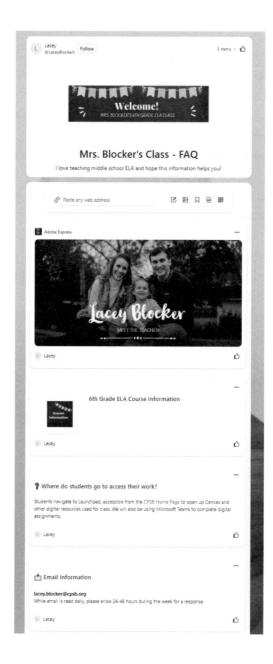

Lacey Blocker, a sixth-grade ISTE Certified ELA Educator, shares a visual link to her Meet the Teacher Adobe page, a link to the course information/syllabus PDF, and general information about the learning units to be covered throughout the year on her public Wakelet page, which is also accessible on her school's teacher website.

Kristie Shaw, a third-grade math teacher, created a public Wakelet page to address her FAQs. The Wakelet is linked on her school's teacher website to provide information and address questions proactively.

For this strategy to be successful, no matter the method by which public information is provided, consider the following best practices.

- Be as useful, yet as general as possible. For example, rather than updating your website each time a new unit begins, provide unit titles with a brief statement to give visitors an idea about what content students are currently learning. If possible, avoid locking in dates and consider using school terms, like semesters or quarters, instead. This way, the information can be used again each year you are teaching the content.

- Take advantage of any features that enable you to control the release of information. Some school websites provide the ability to schedule announcements, with the ability to set a start and end date for the message. Messages that are important all year might have an end date that aligns with the last day of school. This feature allows you to set up messages about school breaks, report card dates, and predetermined standardized testing dates. With this feature, most teachers can knock out a year's worth of announcements in one sitting. Once set up, you can forget about updating for the rest of the year, unless any new information needs to be shared.

- Provide insight about how you arrive at student grades. Knowing that you give weekly quizzes on Friday or the frequency with which homework is assigned is beneficial for parents, guardians, and any tutors the students may use for support.

- Communicate how often student grades are updated. In this 24-7 world, there needs to be reasonable expectations as to when an update can be expected.

- Provide instructions for accessing and a link to where student grades are posted. This step can minimize a multitude of email messages.

- Include your school email address along with your established response expectations, as suggested in chapter 3. This way, if the information being sought remains a question, they can contact you.

- In case visitors arrive at your website after being redirected with your automated email reply, include a reminder of the request you drafted in chapter 3 that asks them to let you know if they find their answer, so you can mark their inquiry as resolved.

- Be consistent. All the strategies you may employ will be for naught if you are not consistent in redirecting students, parents, and others to your teacher website. If the information being requested is available on your website, refrain from repeating information and build capacity and self-sufficiency in your students and others.

- Share how to access your site in as many places as possible. Update your email signature card as explained in chapter 3 and share a hyperlink to your teacher website, along with a QR code for those using mobile devices. QR codes can be posted around the classroom if students have access to devices to scan them. They can also be shared on student take-home folders or any other papers sent home.

- Practice accessing your teacher website with students as soon as possible. By taking this step, you are creating muscle memory for students to become more self-sufficient.

NOTE: When posting information publicly, always protect student privacy and avoid using any personally identifiable information in videos, images, or text.

When using a public hub, it is important to be mindful of student privacy and not include photos, videos, or private student information. **ISTE Standard for Educators 2.3 Citizen** states, "Model and promote management of personal data and digital identity and protect student data privacy." It is always best to err on the side of caution and model good digital citizenship skills.

5-2 Table: Website Creation Tools with Free and Paid Options

Tool	Brief Description	QR Code/Short URL
Adobe Express	Adobe's online resource for creating graphics, online videos, and websites. Free to use when signing up with a school email address.	qr.page/g/3q9iCcK8pWA
Canva	Teachers can sign up for a free educator account with a verifiable school email address to create a multitude of digital content including videos, presentations, posters, websites, and more.	qr.page/g/3DosB8K6RNM
Google Sites	Resource for Google Workspace for Education users.	qr.page/g/3cmvXHzvgoT
Wix	Limited features with a free account. More robust capabilities available with a paid subscription.	qr.page/g/4HzEievhdOu

Tool	Brief Description	QR Code/Short URL
WordPress.com	Create a free website and access templates to use to get started.	qr.page/g/1CiM3sI9Uft

5.5 BECOME A MEDIA PRODUCER

Not everyone aspires to be Sal Khan, the founder of Khan Academy who helped transform education by providing thousands of videos designed to be a resource to help teach students a wide array of educational topics. But the power of video and screen recording should be harnessed by every teacher. Video is the medium of choice for the world in which we live. It is advantageous to have the knowledge and ability to create one's own educational content for students and those who support them.

Videos can be created for a wide variety of reasons including but not limited to:

- lessons to view and review for flipped classrooms, homework purposes, and absent student needs

- instructions for navigating websites or digital resources

- announcements for LMS or digital hub

- substitute content as instructions or to share with students

- video messages

Whether creating videos for flipped classroom lessons or tutorials for students to learn how to navigate your learning management system, here are a few tools to consider.

5-3 Table: Tools for Video Production

Tool	Of Note	QR Code/Short URL
Adobe Express	• free for teachers with a school email address • templates available • videos can be shared with a link or embedded on websites	qr.page/g/2Xh9zoHeJ2F
Canva	• free for teachers with a verifiable educator account • videos can be shared with a link or embedded on websites	qr.page/g/2I9kVlUmvIs
Flip	• currently free for educators • provides screen capture features • provides stickers, backgrounds, and text features • easy to edit • recordings saved in the cloud and shared with a link or embedded on a website	qr.page/g/1VKu5jCahkG

Tool	Of Note	QR Code/Short URL
iOS Screen Recording	• easily captures screen and audio as narration • saves on device, easy to share via iCloud • use Photos app to lightly edit screen recordings • use Clips app to create short videos that can include stickers and text • use iMovie app for heavier editing jobs	qr.page/g/myUsDyGVKQ
Microsoft PowerPoint	• included with Microsoft 365 account • generally, a familiar tool to use • can include video feed narration within presentations • captures annotation • provides screen recording • can export as MP4 to OneDrive to share link or embed from stream	qr.page/g/3Eg2AZBCJpm

Tool	Of Note	QR Code/Short URL
Screencastify	· Chrome extension · can screen record and video record with a webcam · videos stored in cloud to share links or embedded on a website	qr.page/g/1Cm2IolZutC
Windows Photos/ Video Editor Clipchamp	· native Windows app · easy to use—similar to Moviemaker, the fan-favorite from long ago · videos can be edited with text and music features · videos stored in cloud to share with a link or embedded on a website	qr.page/g/4yczZWZ7pPU

5.6 DIGITAL FORMATIVE ASSESSMENTS

One of the most powerful uses of technology in the classroom is in its ability to get real-time formative data from *all* students. Being able to see what students understand, which students need support, and what topics need clarification is transformative in the classroom. No longer do teachers need to give paper quizzes that are hand-graded and returned a few days after the lesson has been taught.

Live feedback during a lesson encourages engagement while measuring understanding at a glance. Tools like Formative, Google Jamboard, Microsoft Whiteboard, Nearpod, Padlet, Pear Deck, and PowerPoint Live all have the power put the lesson in the hands of students, allowing teachers to get to the heart of student understanding in efficient and effective ways.

Google Forms and Microsoft Forms have auto-grading features in quizzes for teachers to customize assessments, and these tools just keep getting better with math editor tools, the ability to scramble questions, options to scramble answers, read-aloud functionality, and translation features. Tools like Gimkit, Kahoot!, and Quizizz deliver similar features in an engaging gamified manner.

Quiz and test features available in learning management systems like Canvas, Google Classroom, Moodle, and Schoology provide the ability to auto-grade assessments, making the grading process much less time-consuming. While there may be a learning curve involved, the time invested is time well spent. As often as possible, and when it is advantageous to the class flow, teachers need to take advantage of digital formative assessment tools. They can make the job of formatively assessing students more efficient, engaging, and effective.

5-4 Table: Digital Formative Assessment Tools

Collaborative Real-Time Formative Assessment Platforms		
Formative	Platform in which teachers can create formative assessments and have students follow along and interact in real time.	qr.page/g/3Q5PH7huWuR
Google Jamboard	Collaborative whiteboard for interactive bell ringers, activities, and exit tickets.	qr.page/g/2cM5JVWNQxX

Microsoft Whiteboard	Digital whiteboard app that teachers can use to set up interactive canvases for students to contribute and collaborate by joining with a link.	qr.page/g/1pWdgK19TQb
Nearpod	Platform that enables teachers to create interactive slide presentations with a wide variety of features that include quizzes, gamified quizzes, multiple choice questions, draw questions, and virtual reality images.	qr.page/g/8fnd5bbiz2
Padlet	Digital board platform that teachers can use to set up collaborative discussions and media sharing via a link or QR code.	qr.page/g/3uWBrXMfL83
Pear Deck	Google Slides and PowerPoint add-on that enables teachers to enhance their presentations with interactive components and have students join sessions.	qr.page/g/PIOctOI9jb
PowerPoint Live	PowerPoint on the web feature that enables teachers to have students follow along in real time with translation feature and limited feedback capability.	qr.page/g/5g2rTroDlAh

Forms, Surveys, and Self-Grading Quiz Formative Assessment Tools Teachers can use these tools to create forms, surveys, and quizzes that can be auto-graded.		
Google Forms		qr.page/g/4tkCLRVgpME
Microsoft Forms		qr.page/g/rjgk9pd16H

Gamified Formative Assessment Tools		
Gimkit	Teachers can create question sets (Kits) that students use to reinforce content in a competitive manner.	qr.page/g/1ZCMjxow4LH
Kahoot!	Game-based learning platform that has ready-made content and provides teachers with the ability to create their own games.	qr.page/g/58q6ThTWXBc
Quizizz	Gamified assessment platform to engage students and provide teachers with a fun way to see what students know.	qr.page/g/14PmiYJeBBA

5.7 STUDENT PEER-TO-PEER COLLABORATION

Often, to the frustration of teachers, students independently harness the power of what some may call "using their resources" or "peer support"—or perhaps "cheating"—when it comes to digital assignments. Whether students are sharing information and pictures of exams in Snapchat groups or "collaborating" on digital assignments, teachers often avoid learning experiences that involve students working together. Perhaps it is time for teachers to avoid the frustration, leverage the potential of peer collaboration, and consider how their formative assignments are structured. The days of assigning end-of-chapter questions or problem sets for students to work through are in the rearview mirror. While the methods students employ to use their available resources to collaborate may vary, they have always been (and likely will always be) a step ahead of teachers when it comes to getting work done.

When we embrace the potential of collaborative formative activities, it benefits both the students and teachers. Students have the chance to learn from one another as they develop their skills. Ultimately, students are responsible for demonstrating proficiency with summative assignments. If, through a collaborative formative process, they develop stronger skills and ability to produce a higher quality summative product, then their learning has been elevated. Consider how few careers have us work in isolation. We rely on support from others to expand and enhance our knowledge and skills. Providing these types of learning experiences benefits students and teachers. Using these types of tools with peer assessments provides students with scaffolded support from their more proficient peers, and teachers benefit from a higher quality summative product from students. Several digital platforms are available to support teachers with this endeavor.

5-5 Table: Tools that Provide Student Peer Collaboration

Tool	Notes	QR Code/Short URL
Classkick	With Classkick, teachers have the ability to deploy assignments and view student work in real time with the additional feature to enable peer support and collaboration.	qr.page/g/CtV7b8mF6X
Google Comments	In Google Docs, Sheets, and Slides, teachers can use comments, action items, and emoji to provide feedback.	qr.page/g/4JIKTO31zox
Microsoft Word Modern Comment Tool	Available in both Word and PowerPoint, students can collaborate, review content, and provide comments on docs and presentations.	qr.page/g/3nDnGlF4WOl
Microsoft Class Teams	A Class Team is a true collaborative space for students to collaborate, communicate, and create content.	qr.page/g/3b6IloT5l6t
Seesaw	This elementary-level platform enables teachers to provide lessons and opportunities for students to create content and to collaborate.	qr.page/g/1bkivBcKCAH

5.8 IT TAKES A VILLAGE

Many free resources are now available for students, parents and guardians, and homework helpers to support the needs of students who are learning at home. For students who may be struggling, providing such resources can support your endeavor in the classroom, lightening your load. Some teachers prefer to create their own video content for reference because it is important for them to ensure student learning is reinforced with the same information provided in the same way in the classroom.

It can be hard for some to relinquish control. But consider the teachers you had throughout your school years. Were they all equally effective at teaching you? It takes a bit of humility to recognize that some of your students might gain a better understanding if the content is delivered and reinforced by a different teacher. If Khan Academy resources had been around when I was a student studying algebra, I would have had less difficulty understanding math concepts. The extra support would have filled the gaps my teachers had not known existed. Opening doors for additional support for students is easier than ever. Here are a few resources available.

Schoolhouse.world

Prompted by student social isolation during the pandemic, Sal Khan (founder of Khan Academy) partnered with his college friend, Shishir Mehrotra (co-founder and CEO of Coda) to develop this free peer-to-peer tutoring service to support students. Schoolhouse.world is now used in more than 100 countries with more than 5,520 tutor volunteers who help students. Students can get live 1:1 support for the following topics:

- pre-algebra, algebra 1, algebra 2, geometry, pre-calculus, calculus, trigonometry, and statistics

- SAT prep

- Indian curriculum including doubt clearing, NTSE preparation, CISCE Board, JEE/NEET Preparation, CBSE classes 9th–12th, and other competitive exams

- AP review for math, science, and computer science

- community support sessions that include new tutor onboarding, game nights, dramatic arts, poetry workshops, and more

- experimental topics in science, computer science, and more, for which there is not yet formal tutoring certification

 Schoolhouse free online tutoring
qr.page/g/2l4BZVEBjMD

TutorMe

TutorMe.com partners with thousands of schools, libraries, and organizations from around the world to provide online 1:1 and on-demand tutoring. Check with your school, district, and library to see if your K–12, higher ed, or military students currently have access. The service is also available for public libraries. Visit their website to contact their support department and request access. K–12 students can schedule tutoring sessions in these subjects:

- math
- science
- English
- social studies
- AP support
- SAT/test prep

 TutorMe
qr.page/g/1zmz3dMBV3t

If neither of the above are a viable option for your students, visit Khan Academy or YouTube, which has educational channels like Crash Course, to see what they have to offer. Reach out to local high schools, universities, and community libraries, which may also provide free services for students.

> As with any online resource, prior to having students sign up (especially with private tutoring services) become familiar with the service's Privacy Policy. Ensure that your students meet the age requirements and that the company adheres to any local, district, or state student privacy. *Always* err on the side of caution. Provide information about the service on your teacher website and disclose if parent permission is required before students access these tutoring resources.

5.9 EXPLORE THE ADVANTAGES OF AI

Artificial Intelligence (AI) has the potential to transform not only education, but also the world. Edtech developers are embracing this technology, as are teachers and students. By the time this book is published, the number of resources available to make teaching tasks more efficient is bound to have grown. According to Maria Walley, cofounder and head of content of Prof Jim, a company that uses AI to transform textbooks into visual experiences, "Using AI, we can eliminate much of the time teachers spend on preparation and grading—reducing their week as much as 30 percent—and giving them more time for what they do best: teach students." (Walley, 2023)

If anyone can figure out how to use a tool for workday advantages, it is teachers. Some ways in which teachers are leveraging the use of ChatGPT include:

- developing personalized writing prompts
- creating rubrics
- assisting with drafting classroom policies
- designing customized classroom content

- planning classroom and school events
- differentiating lessons

AI technology will be incorporated into educational platforms in a number of ways. For example, Microsoft Learning Accelerators are tools integrated into products such as Microsoft Word, PowerPoint, Teams, and more, which can transform the way students learn and build foundational skills.

- *Reading Coach* gives students the opportunity to practice reading, with guidance on pronunciation, syllabification, reading speed, and comprehension.

- *Reading Progress*, available in Microsoft Teams for Education, tracks student progress and gives their teachers actionable insights.

- *Search Coach* helps teachers track students' information literacy skills.

- *Speaker Coach*, available in PowerPoint and Teams, provides real-time feedback to improve speaking skills.

NOTE: Speaker Progress, Math Coach, and Math Progress are anticipated to launch in Microsoft Teams for Education in the 2023–24 school year.

Microsoft Learning Accelerators: tools for students
qr.page/g/4Jtvo3gB4zT

Because of the rapid pace with which this technology is expected to grow, rather than sharing a table of resources and tools, it is likely more beneficial to advise you to search for the most timely and relevant content on social media using these hashtags as a springboard.

- #AIinEDU
- #AIEDU
- #EdTech

As AI technology continues to become a component of educational technology, so does the potential to differentiate instruction, personalize learning experiences, and make the classroom more efficient.

> When teachers design learning experiences to take advantage of tools such as those mentioned in this chapter, it supports **ISTE Standard for Educators 2.5.a**, which suggests that educators "use technology to create, adapt and personalize learning experiences that foster independent learning and accommodate learner differences and needs."

Chapter 5 Reflections on Efficiency

Chapter 5 has introduced a wide range of resources you can use to integrate the strategies described. Take a moment to reflect and jot down some notes to evaluate the strategies and tools, then return to this page when you're ready to integrate them.

Strategy	Notes on Strategy Integration
Automate and Organize Email	
Communicate Effectively	
FAQ Resources as Automated Replies	
Digital Public Self-Serve Hub	
Formative Assessment Tool Integration	

Strategy	Notes on Strategy Integration
Video Production	
Tools for Peer Collaboration	
Leveraging Free Tutoring Services and Coaching Features	
Artificial Intelligence Integration	

Choose and Cultivate Seeds for Efficiency. Use this page to sketch about the strategies you'd like to sow. Consider your expectations for the growth you'll experience, the support and nurturing you'll need from coaches and school leaders; and illustrate how the strategies you choose to implement will positively impact your wellbeing.

Chapter 6

Engagement

"Figuring out new tech to integrate in my lessons is a fun component for me and keeps it interesting as an educator. Being fun and interactive for the students is a bonus."

—Katelyn, a Texas educator with 11–15 years of experience as an educator

OBSERVANT TEACHERS RECOGNIZE WHEN STUDENTS ARE ENGAGED IN learning. Engaged people connect with their experiences, making them more meaningful. The same holds true in one's profession. Engagement with one's work is one of the many keys to unlocking emotional well-being. Remaining curious and excited about teaching and learning is a mindset that can help you feel greater career satisfaction. When we lose interest, we lose enthusiasm. Lack of enthusiasm for learning has a trickle-down effect and dampens student enthusiasm.

Multiple factors come into play when it comes to engagement. Those who have higher intrinsic motivation have an easier time maintaining a high level of engagement. While teachers work diligently to keep learners engaged, they may not work as hard to keep themselves as engaged in teaching. This chapter offers a few suggestions for keeping the teaching flame alive.

6.1 STAY ENERGIZED BY EMERGING TECHNOLOGY

Keeping an eye on emerging technologies helps us envision the future for our students. While there is no way to foresee what classrooms will look like in five, ten, or twenty years, being informed is advantageous for students. Not getting tethered to ideas about the way things used to be and instead getting excited about the potential of things to come brings an engaging energy to the classroom. One way to do this is to remain informed through subscriptions to weekly or monthly newsletters from sources that inform and inspire you. Chapter 4 provided an interactive Padlet activity for readers to share their favorite educational PLN resources. Revisit it to find interesting resources to help you remain energized.

Once you find resources to energize you, subscribe to any newsletters they provide. Then, use the strategy shared in chapter 5 for automating email inboxes. Create a folder and establish a rule to automatically sort the newly subscribed newsletters. This way, you can read them when it's convenient.

> Investments in education and access to technology accelerate progress and change. The **ISTE Standard for Educators 2.1.c** suggests that educators "stay current with research that supports improved student learning outcomes, including findings from the learning sciences."

6.2 EMBRACE PD AS A STUDENT AND AS A TEACHER

Being a lifelong learner means embracing professional development opportunities. Whether they occur in your school, district, or online, approach them with an open mind. A few familiar names in edtech provide outstanding self-paced training paths for teachers to access and are good launching points.

- Apple Education Community

qr.page/g/2UUcKoXPmZh

• Google for Education

 qr.page/g/iXvd4UYGvU

• Microsoft Educator Center

 qr.page/g/183uVHs6xAQ

Perhaps you have knowledge worth sharing or have mastered skills you recognize as valuable for other teachers. It may be a good time to consider offering your own professional development training. Teaching other teachers can be gratifying and reignite the teaching flame or lead you in new directions. Reach out to administrators, coaches, and other personnel to let them know you are ready to lead PD and volunteer to do so.

6.3 INTEGRATE EDTECH TO REMIX TRADITIONAL LESSONS

Beyond daily required lessons, providing students with the opportunity to become creators of ideas and content takes technology integration to the next level and can help spark your imagination and creative side, boosting engagement for you and your students.

Whether you are new to edtech integration or have vast experience with a wide variety of edtech resources, a valuable tool for evaluating how to best integrate technology to support teaching objectives is the Triple E Framework, developed by Dr. Liz Kolb, a clinical associate professor of education technologies and teacher education at the University of Michigan. This framework provides a way for teachers to determine which technology to use to engage, enhance, and extend learning objectives, putting the learning objective first and the technology second. Dr. Kolb's *Learning First, Technology Second in Practice: New Research, New Strategies,*

Research and Tools for Student Success (2020) includes step-by-step processes for edtech coaches and instructional designers to use with teachers for better lesson designs. Meaningful edtech integration comes easier to some than to others. Fortunately, there is the Triple E Framework to use as a tool to help with the process.

 Dr. Liz Kolb's Triple E Framework
qr.page/g/3ntliqE2gwn

When teachers enrich lessons and integrate technology in meaningful ways that are designed to meet the needs of all their students, they support the **ISTE Standard for Educators 2.5 Designer** which suggests that "educators design authentic, learner-driven activities and environments that recognize and accommodate learner variability" and calls for educators to:

- Design authentic learning activities that align with content area standards and use digital tools and resources to maximize active, deep learning (**ISTE Standard for Educators 2.5.b**).

- Explore and apply instructional design principles to create innovative digital learning environments that engage and support learning (**ISTE Standard for Educators 2.5.c**).

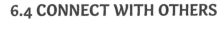 ## 6.4 CONNECT WITH OTHERS

Chapter 4 focused on digital positivity and suggested that you find a professional learning network aligned to your interests to follow. Rather than passively follow or consume what others are sharing, find way to connect with others with similar perspectives and passions. Social media discussion boards and groups are a great place to start getting involved in conversations. If you don't know where to start, use hashtags to help you locate educational topics that interest you. Inevitably, you'll encounter others with the same thoughts and ideas as you, and you may even encounter new and exciting ideas you hadn't yet considered. Finding a group of like-minded individuals can do wonders for feelings of connectedness and improve levels of engagement.

Chapter 6 Reflections on Engagement

Take a moment to reflect upon the suggestions provided in chapter 6.

- This is what *excites* me about edtech . . .

_____

_____

_____

_____

- If I could teach my students *anything*, it would be . . .

_____

_____

_____

_____

- If I could teach my co-teachers *anything*, it would be . . .

_____

_____

_____

_____

- If I could facilitate a digital project on *anything* I teach, I would have students create . . .

  _____

  _____

  _____

  _____

- I benefit from connecting with other teachers to . . .

  _____

  _____

  _____

  _____

Engaging in one's career isn't as simple as flipping a switch. It takes intention, deliberate actions, and time.

Choose and Cultivate Seeds for Engagement. Consider your expectations for the growth you'll experience, the support and nurturing you'll need from coaches and school leaders; and illustrate how the strategies you choose to implement will positively impact your wellbeing.

Chapter 7

Supporting Teachers

The Current State of Education as a Career Choice

Globally, there is a higher demand for teachers than there is a supply—and there is not much evidence to indicate that this will change. According to a press release dated October 4, 2022, the United Nations Educational, Scientific and Cultural Organization (UNESCO) states that within the next decade there will be a global deficit of nearly 69 million teachers. Sub-Saharan Africa is predicted to have the greatest need: to meet the targets set forth by the organization for universal basic education for all by 2030, it will need 5.4 million primary and 11.1 million secondary teachers. With regard to the same target, the press release indicated that Southern Asia is predicted to have a deficit of 1.7 million primary and 5.3 million secondary teachers (UNESCO, 2022).

In the United States, according to the U.S. Department of Labor's Office of Occupational Statistics and Employment Projections, "Overall employment in education, training, and library occupations is projected to grow 7 percent from 2021 to 2031, about as fast as the average for all occupations; this increase is expected to result in about 658,200 new jobs over the decade." (Office of Occupational Statistics and Employment Projections, 2022).

However, it is not easy to determine how critical the teacher shortage may be. In fact, the lack of federal data on this issue is cited as the reason why a team of researchers at the Annenberg Institute for School Reform at Brown University compiled data from a variety of sources including news reports, the Department of Education data, and publicly available information on teacher shortages for every state in the U.S. They found that in 2022, there were 36,000 teaching position vacancies and 163,000 positions being held by underqualified teachers (Nguyen et al., 2022).

And if the projected growth in the education job sector, current vacancies, and lack of qualified teachers are not reasons enough for concern, many current educators are reconsidering their career choice. In January of 2022, the NEA released the results of a survey of 3,621 of its members conducted by the GBA which states, "More than half (55%) of members say they are more likely to leave or retire from education sooner than planned because of the pandemic, almost double the number saying the same in July 2020." (GBA, 2022).

To date, little research has been done on the impact of interventions to foster teacher well-being. According to Dreer & Gouasé:

> "The rapid growth of know-how about brief and effective health programs appears to have not yet found its way into the conceptualization of teacher well-being interventions. As a consequence, it must be concluded that the immense potential of effective and easy-to-implement tools is not yet accessible to the members of a workforce that is known not only for high workloads but also for its high potential in positive social contingency. Considering the digital transformation in schools, which has been catalyzed by the current pandemic crisis, online or blended learning formats will be greatly required in the future of teachers' well-being practice and research. Unfortunately, this review reveals that despite advances in the use of technology for psychological interventions (Riva et al., 2016), digitally assisted well-being interventions for teachers are a rather blank field of research." (Dreer & Gouasé, 2022).

What the research does show is that intervention gains were demonstrated when they addressed teacher stress (Dreer & Gouasé, 2022). Teachers cannot be expected to take care of themselves and reduce their stress in isolation. While most of this book has been written with the teacher in mind as the audience, teacher retention is an effort in which everyone in education should be invested.

Retaining teachers and building capacity with relevant and personalized PD while supporting their effort to improve their emotional well-being is a way to align with **ISTE Standard for Education Leaders 3.1.a,** which suggests that leaders "ensure all students have skilled teachers who actively use technology to meet student learning needs."

School Leader Support for Teachers

A survey conducted by EdWeek Research Center in February of 2022 asked principals and district leaders about the steps they had taken since the pandemic to address the mental health of staff. According to the survey:

- 44% reported that they had offered or increased professional development offerings on self-care

- 33% reported that they had started to make counseling and mental health services available to staff or had added to the services they already offered

- 17% reported that they had not taken any steps to address staff mental health needs despite their current offerings being inadequate

- 15% reported that they had not taken any additional steps because their offerings were already adequate

- 13% added or introduced support groups

- 10% offered staff additional time off

While educational leaders work to "create a culture where teachers and learners are empowered to use technology in innovative ways to enrich teaching and learning" as is suggested by **ISTE Standard for Education Leaders 3.3 Empowering Leader**, considerations need to be made by all who work with teachers.

TECH SUGGESTIONS FOR LEADERS TO PROMOTE TEACHER WELL-BEING

- Keep instructional disruptions to a minimum and schedule announcements so that the same classes are not always the ones being disrupted.

- Respect planning periods. Encourage teachers to add their planning periods to any shared digital calendars and avoid scheduling extra tasks for them during this time.

- Streamline email correspondence.

- Limit the number of email messages sent per day or week.

- Keep the email messages clear and concise, minimizing cognitive load.

- Send messages *only* to those for whom the message is intended. Use the bcc field if concerned about the privacy of recipients.

- Provide a way for teachers to access digital forms and information on their own, eliminating the need to email someone else to retrieve and send to them. This can be done with a shared folder with read-only access.

- Instead of frequent meetings, consider posting video messages with updates and information for teachers to check weekly.

- Provide time for teachers to collaborate on lesson development and address student needs together.

- Recognize and encourage teachers when they overcome obstacles.

By its nature, education is an environment in which people are moving at different rates and in different directions. Giving teachers access to information at times best suited to their own needs should be considered when possible. While some information may need to be communicated immediately, the ability for teachers to access information when best suited to their schedule demonstrates a respect for their time. Consistency is also appreciated; muscle memory of routine tasks helps prevent feelings of technostress.

Wellness Initiatives around the World

School systems are beginning to take teacher wellness initiatives more seriously. The article "3 Wellbeing Initiatives That Work for Schools" on the Tech & Learning website describes how Downers Grove South High School in Illinois makes well-being a priority with Mindfulness Mondays, where 450 teachers and staff members have access to guided meditations facilitated by a specialized counselor and have access to a free subscription to a mindfulness app (Ullman, 2022). Districts and schools have also started to employ school wellness coordinators who focus on the overall well-being of a school population. Their role is to evaluate the needs of students and staff, then develop a plan for improvement, because positive work environments promote productivity and foster trust and satisfaction (Zuger, 2023).

In February 2023, Representative Suzanne Bonamici (D-OR-1) introduced a US Congressional bill, H.R. 744—Supporting the Mental Health of Educators and Staff Act of 2023, that if passed, would establish grants and require other activities "to improve mental and behavioral health among education professionals and other school staff." Additionally, the bill would require the Department of Health and Human Services (HHS) to "study and develop policy recommendations on:

- improving mental and behavioral health among education professionals and other school staff,
- removing barriers to accessing care and treatment, and
- identifying strategies to promote resiliency."

The topic of teacher wellness has become a global issue. Governmental efforts to support the emotional welfare of educators have the potential to effect change. In October 2022, The World Economic Forum reported four takeaways from a discussion they held on World Teachers' Day to talk about the importance of teacher wellness in a post-pandemic world:

1. There will be no learning recovery without well prepared, appreciated, and empowered teachers.

2. Teacher well-being depends not only on their working conditions but also their own sense of self-efficacy.

3. There are cost-effective, focused interventions to enhance teachers' well-being.

Teachers' well-being and their voice should be front and center of efforts to recover learning and build back resilient, equitable, and effective education systems. (Ding et al., 2022)

General Support of Teacher Well-being

While leaders and legislators shape policy, *everyone* can support teacher well-being. Here are a few suggestions for how to support teachers as they prioritize their own mental health from Mental Health America (Mental Health America, 2023):

- check in on teachers to see how they are doing
- keep them accountable for their own self-care
- express gratitude
- laugh with them

- pay attention to their nonverbal cues
- offer your support

Just as teachers should be comfortable asking for what they need, school leaders and changemakers must not overlook the inclusion of teacher input regarding the ways in which they need support. Cultivating a global culture where teachers feel heard, valued, and supported promotes the well-being of all.

Appendix A

Overview of Tech Strategies for Teacher Wellness

Well-Being
2

2.1
I am self-aware.

2.2
I practice daily self-care.

2.3
I practice mindfulness.

2.4
I make time for daily deep breathing exercises.

2.5
I seek support when needed.

Boundaries
3

3.1
I guard my personal phone number.

3.2
I redirect, identify, and block phone numbers.

3.3
I keep my work email separate from my personal email.

3.4
I establish and communicate email response expectations.

3.5
I use email response features.

3.6
I manage digital notifications.

Digital Positivity
4

4.1
I know my social media audience.

4.2
I avoid the algorithm of negativity.

4.3
I adjust my social media feeds for my emotional well-being.

4.4
I tap into the power of positivity.

4.5
I recognize growth with gratitude.

4.6
I cultivate digital kindness.

Efficiency
5

5.1
I use automated email features.

5.2
I provide FAQs as automated responses.

5.3
I communicate student expectations effectively.

5.4
I maintain a public teacher website.

5.5
I create my own video content to share with others.

5.6
I take advantage of digital formative assessment features.

5.7
I provide students with peer-to-peer collaboration opportunities.

5.8
I share tutoring resources with students.

5.9
I explore how AI can positively impact my workflow.

Engagement
6

6.1
I stay informed about emerging technologies.

6.2
I embrace PD as a student and as a teacher.

6.3
I use edtech to engage, enhance, and extend learning.

6.4
I use technology to actively connect with others.

Appendix B

Educator Resources

While specific websites for resources referenced throughout the book have been provided in context with websites and QR codes, digital locations for information changes frequently. This section contains more general website locations that can be searched for specific topics if any of the QR codes or website addresses should become unavailable.

Adobe Express for Education—adobe.com/education/express

Android Digital Wellbeing—android.com/digital-well-being

Apple Education Community—education.apple.com

Apple Support—support.apple.com

Canva for Education—canva.com/education

Classkick—classkick.com

Education Support, U.K.—educationsupport.org.uk

Facebook Help Center—facebook.com/help

Flip—info.flip.com

Formative—training.formative.com

Gimkit—gimkit.com/

Google Support—support.google.com

Headspace for Educators—headspace.com/educators

HelpGuide.org—helpguide.org/find-help.htm

Instagram Help Center—help.instagram.com

Kahoot!—kahoot.com

Mental Health America—mhanational.org

Pear Deck Content Orchard—peardeck.com/content-orchard

Microsoft Educator Center—learn.microsoft.com/en-us/training/educator-center

Microsoft Support—support.microsoft.com

Nearpod—nearpod.com

Padlet—padlet.com

Quizizz—quizizz.com

Schoolhouse—schoolhouse.world

Screencasitfy—screencastify.com

Seesaw—web.seesaw.me

TikTok Support—support.tiktok.com

TutorMe—tutorme.com

Wix—wix.com

WordPress.com—wordpress.com/create

Glossary

algorithm: A step-by-step procedure for solving a problem or accomplishing some end.

autonomy: Self-directing freedom and especially moral independence.

box breathing: A pattern of deep breathing that calls for four seconds of inhalation, four seconds of holding breath, four seconds of exhalation, and a four-second pause before repeating the cycle two or three more times.

burnout: Exhaustion of physical or emotional strength or motivation, usually as a result of prolonged stress or frustration.

doomscrolling: Scrolling through content that elicits negative emotions.

locus of control: The perception of what controls the outcomes in one's life. The perception of an external locus of control is associated with a sense of helplessness over outcomes. The perception of an internal locus of control is associated with the sense that one has control over their life outcomes.

mindfulness: The practice of maintaining a nonjudgmental state of heightened or complete awareness of one's thoughts, emotions, or experiences on a moment-to-moment basis.

mindset theory: Carol Dweck's theory that one develops either a "growth" or "fixed" mindset. A growth mindset is associated with a sense of control over one's ability to grow and learn. A fixed mindset is associated with a sense that one's growth and learning abilities are unchanging.

occupational stress: Stress that is associated with one's occupation, derived from the sense that one cannot fully meet the expectations of one's duties.

self-awareness: An awareness of one's own personality or individuality.

self-care: Care for oneself to promote wellness.

Sketchnoting: Doodling or drawing ideas from learned content.

social-emotional learning (SEL): An educational method to foster the social and emotional development of the learner.

techno-anxiety: Anxiety elicited by the use of technology or the lack of knowledge when using it.

techno-fatigue: Fatigue prompted by the use of technology sometimes referred to as information overload or digital fatigue.

technostress: Stress that is attributed by feelings of techno-anxiety and/or techno-fatigue.

References/Bibliography

Blank, R. (2023). Social media algorithms & your mental well-being. *Healthier Tech*. www. healthiertech.co/social-media-algorithms/.

Carroll, A., York, A., Fynes-Clinton, S., Sanders-O'Connor, E., Flynn, L., Bower, J. M., Forrest, K., & Ziaei, M. (2021). The downstream effects of teacher well-being programs: Improvements in teachers' stress, cognition and well-being benefit their students. *Frontiers in Psychology*, *12*. doi. org/10.3389/fpsyg.2021.689628

Collaborative for Academic, Social, and Emotional Learning. (2022, March 11). *Fundamentals of SEL*. CASEL. casel.org/fundamentals-of-sel

Cruz, M. C. (2021). *Risk. Fail. Rise.: A teacher's guide to learning from mistakes*. Heinemann.

Ding, E., Arias, O., Mijares, A. & Molina, E. (2022, October 20). For better learning outcomes, we must prioritize teacher well-being. *Weforum*. weforum.org/agenda/2022/10/ teachers-well-being-and-empowerment-learning-recovery-acceleration

Dreer, B., & Gouasé, N. (2021). Interventions fostering well-being of schoolteachers: A Review of Research. *Oxford Review of Education*, *48*(5), 587–605. doi.org/10.1080/03054985.2021.2002290

Dweck, C. S., & Leggett, E. L. (1988). A social-cognitive approach to motivation and personality. *Psychological Review*, *95*(2), 256–273. doi.org/10.1037/0033-295x.95.2.256

Estrada-Muñoz, C., Castillo, D., Vega-Muñoz, A., & Boada-Grau, J. (2020). Teacher Technostress in the Chilean School System. *International Journal of Environmental Research and Public Health*, *17*(15), 5280. doi.org/10.3390/ijerph17155280

Fan, R. (2021, April 30). Teaching is not martyrdom. *Psychology Today*. www.psychologytoday.com/ us/blog/social-emotional-learning-teachers/202104/teaching-is-not-martyrdom

Fernández-Batanero, J.-M., Román-Graván, P., Reyes-Rebollo, M.-M., & Montenegro-Rueda, M. (2021). Impact of educational technology on teacher stress and anxiety: A literature review. *International Journal of Environmental Research and Public Health*, *18*(2), 548. doi. org/10.3390/ijerph18020548

GBAO. (2022, January 31). *Poll results: Stress and burnout pose threat of educator shortages*. NEA. nea.org/sites/default/files/2022-02/NEA%20Member%20COVID-19%20Survey%20Summary.pdf

Gonzalez, J. (2013, August 29). *Find your marigold: The one essential rule for new teachers*. Cult of Pedagogy. cultofpedagogy.com/marigolds/

H.R.744—118th Congress (2023-2024): Supporting the Mental Health of Educators and Staff Act of 2023. (2023, February 10). congress.gov/bill/118th-congress/house-bill/744

Hopper, S. 1., Murray, S. L., Ferrara, L. R., & Singleton, J. K. (2019). Effectiveness of diaphragmatic breathing for reducing physiological and psychological stress in adults. *JBI Database of Systematic Reviews and Implementation Reports, 17*(9), 1855–1876. doi.org/10.11124/jbisrir-2017-003848

International Barometer of Education. (2023, February 10). Education and Solidarity Network. educationsolidarite.org/en/our-actions/international-barometer-of-the-health-and-well-being-of-education-personnel/

Kolb, L. (2017). *Learning first, technology second: The educator's guide to designing authentic lessons*. International Society for Technology in Education.

Kolb, L. (2020, December 9). Triple E Framework. tripleeframework.com/

Leichtman, K. (2022, May 26). *How burned out are you? A scale for teachers*. Edutopia. edutopia.org/article/how-burned-out-are-you-scale-teachers/

Mind Garden. (2023). *Maslach Burnout Inventory (MBI)—assessments, tests*. Mind Garden. mindgarden.com/117-maslach-burnout-inventory-mbi

Nash, J. (2018, January 5). *How to set healthy boundaries & build positive relationships*. PositivePsychology.com. positivepsychology.com/great-self-care-setting-healthy-boundaries/

Satici, S. A., Gocet Tekin, E., Deniz, M. E., & Satici, B. (2022). Doomscrolling scale: Its association with personality traits, psychological distress, social media use, and well-being. *Applied Research in Quality of Life*. doi.org/10.1007/s11482-022-10110-7

Sussex Publishers. (2023). *Mindfulness*. Psychology Today. psychologytoday.com/us/basics/mindfulness

Terada, Y. (2021, August 21). *Defending a Teacher's Right to Disconnect*. Edutopia. edutopia.org/article/defending-teachers-right-disconnect

Tikkanen, L., Pyhältö, K., Soini, T., & Pietarinen, J. (2021). Crossover of burnout in the classroom—is teacher exhaustion transmitted to students? *International Journal of School & Educational Psychology, 9*(4), 326–339. doi.org/10.1080/21683603.2021.1942343

Ullman, E. (2022, December 13). *3 wellbeing initiatives that work for schools*. Techlearning. techlearning.com/news/3-wellbeing-initiatives-that-work-for-schools

U.S. Bureau of Labor Statistics. (2022, September 8). *Education, training, and Library Occupations: Occupational outlook handbook*. bls.gov/ooh/education-training-and-library/home.htm

U.S. Department of Education Office of Educational Technology. (2023, January 23). *Funding digital learning*. tech.ed.gov/funding/

U.S. Department of Education Office of Inspector General. (2022, September 26). *Allocation of ESSER I funds at selected local educational agencies*. oversight.gov/report/ED/Allocation-ESSER-I-Funds-Selected-Local-Educational-Agencies

U.S. Department of Education. (2023, February 15). *Elementary and Secondary School Emergency Relief Fund*. Office of Elementary and Secondary Education. oese.ed.gov/offices/education-stabilization-fund/elementary-secondary-school-emergency-relief-fund/

UNESCO. (2022, October 4). *World Teachers' Day: UNESCO sounds the alarm on the global teacher shortage crisis*. unesco.org/en/articles/world-teachers-day-unesco-sounds-alarm-global-teacher-shortage-crisis?hub=701

Van Katwyk, P. T., Fox, S., Spector, P. E., & Kelloway, E. K. (2000). Using the job-related affective well-being scale (JAWS) to investigate affective responses to work stressors. *Journal of Occupational Health Psychology, 5*(2), 219–230. doi.org/10.1037/1076-8998.5.2.219

Walley, M. (2023, February 1). Teachers are burning out. Can AI help?. Eschoolnews. eschoolnews.com/digital-learning/2023/02/01/teachers-are-burning-out-can-ai-help/

Will, M., & Superville, D. R. (2022, June 9). *Don't forget the adults: How schools and districts can support educator mental health*. Education Week. edweek.org/teaching-learning/dont-forget-the-adults-how-schools-and-districts-can-support-educator-mental-health/2022/03

Zuger, S. (2023, April 11). *School wellness coordinators: What to know*. Techlearning. techlearning.com/news/wellness-coordinators-what-to-know

Illustration Credits

Illustrations created by Meredith Masar Boullion using Canva for Educators.

Index